# IN QUEST OF WHOLENESS

# IN QUEST OF WHOLENESS

*Essays & Dialogues*

Thomas Hora, M.D.

The PAGL Foundation
Old Lyme, Connecticut

*Permissions:*

We wish to express gratitude for permission to reprint the following articles, all by Thomas Hora: "Cognition and Health," *Journal of Religion and Health* 1, no. 3 (April 1962); "Religious Values in Illness and Health," *Journal of Religion and Health* 2, no. 3 (April 1963) (the *Journal of Religion and Health* is a publication of the Academy of Religion and Health); "Beyond Self," *Psychologia* 5, no. 2, Kyoto, Japan (June 1962); "The Transpersonal Perspective," *American Journal of Psychoanalysis* 23, no. 1 (May 1963); "Discussion of Dr. Hulbeck's Paper: Three Creative Phases in Psychoanalysis," *American Journal of Psychoanalysis* 23, no. 2 (November 1963); "Responsibilty," *Review of Existential Psychology and Psychiatry* 2, no. 3 (Fall 1962); "The Epistemology of Love," *Journal of Existential Psychiatry* 2, no. 7 (Winter 1962); "Transcendence and Healing," *Journal of Existential Psychiatry* 1, no. 4 (1961); "Existential Psychotherapy, Basic Principles," in *Current Therapies*, vol. 2, ed. J. H. Masserman (New York: Grune and Stratton, 1962).

Printed in the United States of America

Third edition, 2002

ISBN 1-931052-00-X

# Contents

# Foreword to the Third Edition

It has been more than thirty years since these papers were first published and distributed among students of Dr. Hora eager to search deeper into consciousness than conventional therapy ventured. Subsequent to initial publication there have been several more books and booklets, as well as tapes of seminars and conferences.

Those who have continued to study these materials have seen the evolution of ideas from a rudimentary departure from traditional psychotherapeutic ideas to an altogether unique teaching, later called metapsychiatry.

Reading these papers is like following the river to the headwaters, the bubbling stream of inspiration fresh with discovery and bold with expressive clarity. But no matter whether one studies the later more developed ideas or the earlier seminal thoughts, both imbue the student with vital, spiritual nourishment fresh from the Source.

JAN LINTHORST
IRVINE, CALIFORNIA
OCTOBER 2002

# Foreword

This is the second time that Dr. Hora's essays and dialogues have been collected. The first time they sold out quickly and travelled practically throughout the world, being frequently reprinted, quoted in the literature, and used by professional and lay people as a source of learning, healing and personal growth.

The book consists of published and unpublished articles and lectures that have been in private circulation among various groups and individuals for over ten years. The writings reflect the trend of one man's thinking about human existence and psychotherapeutic knowledge.

Great scientists have always been seekers after the truth. Advanced thinkers often transcend their particular frames of reference in quest of broader and deeper understanding of Reality. In this book it is a psychiatrist who goes beyond the confines of traditional thought to discover the truth about man and his place in the universe.

Starting with the traditional schools of psychoanalysis, the author's search for understanding led him through Jung, Heidegger, Binswanger and other European existentialists to the study of Eastern existentialism and Oriental religions. These, in turn, led him to new insights about the spiritual and existential meanings of biblical thought, notably the teachings of Jesus. Out of this rich and varied background he developed a psychotherapeutic perspective oriented toward health and enlightenment, rather than toward illness and pathogenesis.

A beginning break through the traditional patterns of psychotherapeutic thinking is noticeable in the shift of emphasis from the concept of causality to the concept of "modes of being-in-the-world." Traditionally, a patient was viewed within the limits of the biophysiological and the socio-environmental context, wherein the determining causes of illness were assumed to lie. The author,

in seeking to discover and identify the nature of health, has come
to view human existence from a broader perspective. This is the
ontic perspective, which includes not only the physical, emotional
and intellectual spheres, but also the transcendental dimension of
man's reality. This transcendent, existential-spiritual dimension is
central to Dr. Hora's view, in which it is precisely the individual's
realization of life in its ultimate dimension that brings healing.
This realization restores the integrity of the individual's being and
brings him into harmony with the Fundamental Order of Existence. Illness then is seen not as evidence that the individual is lack-
ing, or is warped or diseased in his being, but as a manifestation
of a "mode of being" that is misdirected. It is not the "stuff" of
life that is wanting, but the "way" in which the individual is going about living his life. Healing is a consequence of understanding oneself ontically, of seeing one's life in an existential context.
The author calls it "ontic" integration.

In the essays "Cognition and Health" and "Wholeness" we
find a clear statement of the principle that cognition determines
man's mode of being. The author shows that the task of the therapist is to help the patient to understand the language of his symptoms as silent communications about his misdirected modes of
being-in-the-world. The relevance of thinking to being is thus highlighted. A misdirected consciousness can be recognized as the
source of disharmonies of existence. By "knowing rightly" one can
attain a mode of being that leads to wholesome and harmonious
life experiences.

In line with this principle, the author develops certain new categories of thought for both everyday life and for therapeutic practice. One such category is the loving and reverent mode of cognition. Nobody will dispute that a loving attitude favorably
influences the therapeutic process, but "the loving and reverent
mode of cognition" is more than a technique. It frees the mind
from conceptual interferences, enabling the therapist to pay undivided attention to that which is unfolding in the present. This
is a phenomenological perception. It goes beyond technique and
makes possible a clear discernment of man's mode of being-in-the-
world. The essay on "The Epistemology of Love" presents the
very core of therapy and the basic conditions of healing.

The author's contact with Eastern religious thought has re-
sulted in still another development, namely, the clarification of the

issue of overcoming the subject/object dichotomy. Such transcendence is known to be an important aspect of Zen training. For centuries Zen masters, realizing higher levels of consciousness and awareness, have guided their students, by way of confrontation with paradoxical logic, to the experience of freedom from bondage to dualistic ways of thinking, whether pictorial, sensory, emotional or intellectual. The insights gained from the Zen tradition are developed in the essays "Beyond Self," "Responsibility," and "The Transpersonal Perspective."

One such insight is the concept of "personhood," so highly valued in Western cultures, which is, in effect, a fountainhead of diseases and discordant conditions. The sense of personhood can be overcome by "recognizing personal and interpersonal phenomena as being merely conceptual in character." The question arises, What then does constitute the true individual? What is the essence of man's being? In the essay on "Identity" the author describes authentic man as a translucent medium and a presence that reflects the qualities of Existence. The quality of man's presence is determined by his values such as integrity, intelligence and love. Enlightened man is seen as a "beneficial presence" in the world. This concept is presented throughout the book in various ways. The quality of a healthy man's presence is seen as springing from a consciousness characterized by intelligence, honesty, reverence, attentiveness, love and serenity. Such consciousness is at one with the fundamental principles governing Existence and is therefore open to the source of life that manifests itself in health and harmony.

The Buddhists speak of this state and quality of consciousness as the "attainment of Buddhahood." In the Bible this may be found in the injunction of Paul, *"Let this mind be in you, which was also in Christ Jesus"* (Phil. 2:5). The analogy of Buddhahood and Christhood has shed much light on the teachings of Jesus. It highlights Jesus' role as a healer and the relevance of his teachings to the issues of health. In the essays on "Prayer," God is defined as the Harmonizing Principle of Existence, reflected by man in spiritual qualities and values. Thus, the void left by the absence of limiting assumptions and the concept of "personhood" is filled with the presence of existential qualities and values, which are transpersonal in character. The individual, liberated from self-confirming tendencies, becomes one with the Principle of Life and draws vitality, intelligence and love from this source beyond himself. By participating in life as an enlightened, beneficial presence, man attains wholeness.

*"Blessed are they which do hunger and thirst after righteousness: for they shall be [ful]filled"* (Matt. 5:6).

JAN LINTHORST, EDITOR
GARDEN GROVE, CALIFORNIA
SPRING 1972

# Cognition and Health

This is an age of mass communication. It is also an age when ideological conflicts and mental diseases are appearing on an unprecedented scale throughout the world. It appears that contemporary man lives in an increasingly polluted atmosphere, in a *noosphere*[1]—that is, a mental climate—that is more or less overcharged and harmful.

This mental climate consists of explicit or implicit, overt or covert, consciously or paraconsciously communicated thoughts, ideologies, affects, values, and meanings, which fill the culture of a nation, community, family groups or dyadic situations. Paraconscious perception and communication is the transmission of messages among individuals and groups without premeditated intention on the part of the senders and/or without conscious awareness on the part of the receivers.

Categories of thought and systems of values greatly determine the limits of human cognition. The biblical view of man, *"For as he thinketh in his heart, so is he"* (Prov. 23:7), can be elaborated into a realization that as a man thinketh, so does he see, so does he act, react, respond. Through his behavior and countenance man conveys his thoughts, values, and basic assumptions. These thoughts, values, and preconceptions communicate themselves either consciously or paraconsciously and tend to elicit various reactions depending on whether they reinforce or clash with the thoughts and values of those within reach. The cognitive and behavioral consequences of categories of thought and systems of values can be observed on the social level, in family settings, or in dyadic situations.

In a society where competitiveness is overemphasized, for instance, the mental climate tends to become cruel and nihilating. In such a culture interhuman communion is made difficult, and love impossible. Jealousies, power struggles, greed, and mutually competitive negations alienate people from each other and lead to progressive disintegration of social life and corresponding increases in mental illness.

In one community, for instance, a group of wealthy parents were shocked to see their children arrested for theft and robbery, in spite of the fact that they had showered them with everything they desired. In exploring the family climate it was discovered, however, that these parents placed great value on acquisitions and on successful business and market operations. The children, having absorbed these values, proceeded to act them out in ways that were socially unacceptable.

In another family, a young man became a homosexual to the great consternation of his respectable parents. Yet when the situation was explored, it was revealed that the boy was striving to live up to his parents' exaggerated concern with the importance of being masculine, beyond any suspicion of showing so-called sissy tendencies. To this boy homosexuality was a way of "practicing" what his parents "preached": He was asserting his own masculinity over other less "masculine" males.

In dyadic situations the preconscious perception of patients in psychoanalytic treatment has been described by Jan Ehrenwald as "doctrinal compliance." It consists of the curious fact that patients tend to provide their analysts with dreams and free associations that fit the doctors' particular frame of reference and personal theoretical bias. "Freudian patients" tend to have Freudian dreams, "Jungian patients" Jungian dreams, and so on.

One of the consequences of the Cartesian subject-object perspective on life is that man is viewed as a separated, self-contained monad, wrapped in his skin, the contents of which need therapeutizing. The image of man is often that of a package filled with aggression and lust.

Some observers have endeavored to rationalize the preponderance of crime and violence in the movies and on television psychoanalytically, asserting that they are good for the public because they provide an opportunity for vicarious discharge of the pent-up hostilities and impulses that everyone supposedly has "inside" himself. Unfortunately, mental health statistics and the alarming rise of juvenile delinquency and criminality provide a sad proof of the mistake inherent in the concept of vicarious discharge of hostilities.

This example represents but one of the consequences of the erroneous view of man fostered by scientific objectification. For it is becoming clear that the more hostility is being "discharged," the more there is of it. Man is not a container of impulses and drives; neither is he an energy system in terms of the combustion engine, nor is he an analogue computer. Man is a spiritual being, that is, a creative mind intimately related to his world and cognitively responsive (responsible) to it.

Cognition and consciousness are essential elements of human existence. They are subject to ideological influences reaching man through many channels of communication. Ideas cannot be discharged like trash from a can; ideas need to be understood and confronted with reality. Truth is the only solvent and annihilator of false ideas, just as light is the only remedy for darkness. *"Ye shall know the truth and the truth shall make you free"* (Jn. 8:32). It is truth and understanding that liberate man from his misguided notions and hostilities, not the gratification of them. Man does not produce truth; he is rather a "translucent medium of Existence"—that is, he manifests truth and is defined by it.

Commercialism, advertising, political and religious propaganda are made possible by man's inclination to absorb messages and to become an unaware victim of preconscious perceptions and subliminal influences. The advent of the electronic media of mass communication has made this a major mental health hazard.

There is, for instance, considerable justification for the view that the publicizing of diseases leads to more harm than good, because it creates paraconscious relations in the form of anxiety states, hypochondriacal concerns, and psychosomatic phenomena.

Today the psychiatrist cannot dismiss the paranoid patient's anxieties about being "influenced" as mere psychopathology and projective mental mechanisms. Today the question is not whether it is realistic to claim that one is being influenced, but rather how to remain capable of withstanding all the influences that increasingly impinge upon human consciousness. In other words, how is man to retain his psychological and spiritual integrity in a noosphere that is becoming increasingly dense and polluted?

## BRAINWASHING

The term *brainwashing* is a misnomer when applied to the political indoctrination of prisoners, since any kind of indoctrination is an endeavor to fill the mind with certain ideological content rather than to "wash" it clean. The minds of men have become battlefields where ideologies and commercial interests are at war with one another. It is therefore of the utmost importance to find a way of safeguarding the integrity and epistemological freedom of human consciousness. In other words, if mental health—that is, the sanity of the world—is to be preserved, man must learn, so to speak, to "wash his own brain clean" and keep it so, in spite of the toxic influences contained in the mental climate in which he must live.

The contemporary philosopher Martin Heidegger recommends "Gelassenheit zu den Dingen,"[2] which, in essence, is an attitude of mental nonattachment to whatever may commend itself to human consciousness as overly important.

Perhaps the most radical defense against mental contamination, which could also be considered a method of self-administered therapeutic brainwashing, is meditation, as practiced and taught in Zen Buddhism.

Interestingly enough, the meditation methods practiced in Zen were discovered, practiced, and taught five thousand years ago by the Taoist sages. *Mind-fasting*[3] is a term derived from the translation of a Chinese text that deals with the advice given by the Taoist sage Chuang-tzu to his disciple Yen Hui. In instructing his disciple, Chuang-tzu said: "When you listen with the ears, do not hear with your ears, and when you listen with the mind, do not hear with the mind. Listen with the spirit so that you can hear with the spirit."

Jesus is also known to have recommended to his disciples *"prayer and fasting"* (Matt. 17:21) in order to gain the higher levels of faith, wisdom, and enlightenment that would enable them to be more effective in their healing missions. Prayer and fasting may have meant, analogously, meditation and mind-fasting, that is, abstaining from hearing with the ears and with the mind in order to become capable of hearing with the spirit.

The following passages from the book of Matthew (13:10-17) seem highly relevant to the epistemological problems connected with man's cognitive faculties:

Verse 10  *And the disciples came, and said unto him, why speakest thou to them in parables?*

Verse 11  *He answered and said unto them, because it is given unto you to know the mysteries of the kingdom of heaven, but to them it is not given.*

Verse 14 *And in them is fulfilled the prophesy of Esaias, which saith, by hearing you shall hear and shall not understand; and seeing you shall see, and shall not perceive.*

Verse 15 *For this people's heart is waxed gross, and their ears are dull of hearing, and their eyes they have closed; lest at any time they should see with their eyes, and hear with their ears, and should understand with their heart and should be converted, and I should heal them.*

Verse 16 *But blessed are your eyes, for they see: and your ears, for they hear.*

Verse 17 *For verily I say unto you, that many prophets and righteous men have desired to see those things which ye see, and have not seen them, and to hear those things which ye hear, and have not heard them.*

In considering these ancient recommendations from the standpoint of cognitive integration, we cannot help but marvel at the insight they reveal about the human mind and human existence. For instance, Chuang-tzu actually revealed and taught the differentiation of three levels of human cognition which correspond to three dimensions of consciousness. These, in turn, underlie three different modes of being-in-the-world, that is, three modes (levels, dimensions) of cognitive integration.

## DIMENSIONS OF COGNITIVE INTEGRATION

From the standpoint of man's contact with the world around him we can differentiate three modes of perception that roughly correspond to Chuang-tzu's description of mind-fasting:

1. fascination, which is mostly sensory;
2. concentration, which involves the intellect; and
3. attention, which is a higher modality of integrated awareness.

The child is fascinated by a sound or by a shining object purely on the basis of hearing with his ears or seeing with his eyes, without reasoning about it or comprehending what it is. The intellectual tends to speculate, compare, judge, evaluate, and think about what he perceives. He ends with an interpretation of what the thing should be in accordance with his pre-existing categories of knowledge. The attentive man receives the percept in its essence, and comprehends its actual reality.

Fascination is nonrational contact with the outside world. Concentration is a rational or an irrational mode of rationalizing about a percept. Attention is neither rational nor irrational. It is real. It receives that which reveals itself as it is. Fascination, then, is sensory; concentration is intellectual; and attention is spiritual, that is, a loving mode of cognition. Fascination tends to elicit affective reactions. Concentration leads to interpretative reasoning. Attention results in an understanding-loving response to that which reveals itself.

The man who perceives with his senses alone tends to react; he is usually personal in his reactions. The intellectually perceiving man is inclined toward influencing the environment; his is an interpersonal mode of acting. Loving man is concerned with neither the personal nor the interpersonal aspects of experience; rather, he is concerned with understanding and perceiving the truth. His perspective transcends the person: his is a transpersonal perspective.

The man who "listens with his ears" is in bondage to his environment, somewhat as animals are. His existence revolves mostly around sensory and affective stimulation. Thinking man—who "listens with his mind"—is in bondage to his self-image, to his preconceived notions, to his calculating tendencies: He tends to be concerned about being right or wrong, good or bad. Loving man—who "listens with the spirit"—is free, for he is in contact and in harmony with reality, and sees the truth of what is.

Looking at human beings from this perspective, we can broadly distinguish three modes of being-in-the-world and correspondingly we can differentiate three types of man: the prevalently sensuous, the prevalently intellectual, and the loving man.


## SENSUOUS MAN

Sensuous man seeks the meaning of existence in pleasurable sensations. The world is, so to speak, his "apple pie." For him, eating often serves as entertainment, sex is essentially masturbation, and he tends to "eat words" rather than understand their meaning. He has an "alimentary approach" to life and seeks to "digest" whatever he encounters. He either "takes things in" or "spits them out." He is inclined to think in terms of accepting or rejecting. Whatever he accepts, however, undergoes an adulteration process. This is manifested in a tendency to misinterpret, misquote, and defile what has been "taken in." Man who holds the "alimentary world view" is prone to gastrointestinal somatizations such as butterfly sensations in the stomach, gastric complications, and various forms of intestinal diskynesias.

This mode of existence brings with it a world image consisting of two realms, the inside and the outside, separated from each other by a wrapping of skin that has entrance and exit holes of communication. This dualistic mental image has far reaching consequences inasmuch as it conditions man's mode of being-in-the-world, as well as how he experiences existence. It certainly interferes with the realization of transcendence and the at-one-ment of the realm of Love, which is beyond the duality of inside/outside.

Sensuous man quite often tends to enjoy the sensations of talking and being talked to. He is concerned with sensory gratification rather than with understanding. He engages in conversation without communicating. He talks "just for the fun of it." Echolalia may be considered an extreme example of speech used for sensory gratification. Sensuous man may spend years in psychotherapy without ever being touched by it, unless his mode of being-in-the-world is phenomenologically elucidated. Or he may graduate from college without having learned anything. Or he may strive to "use" religion, God, and the community for personal emotional gratification. The sensuous man considers himself either the beneficiary or the butt of the world.

## INTELLECTUAL MAN

Strangely enough, one of the major dilemmas of intellectual man stems from his striving "to be good" to his fellow man. This goodness, however, is the product of thinking. For him, goodness, as behavior, is a calculated affair. Calculated behavior is inevitably experienced by others as manipulation. To be the object of manipulation is a more or less debasing experience. The recipient of such goodness is invariably in a "double bind": He is being benefited and patronized (belittled) at the same time. His reason demands that he be grateful, but his self-esteem demands revolt. He must repress the temptation to rebel in order to appear rational.

Suppressed revolt tends to become simmering rage, embarrassment, helpless fury. This condition may lead to depressions, acting out, or resorting to drugs or alcohol.

Such goodness, in a sense, is more pernicious than badness or meanness. Meanness justifies a hostile response. The victim of human badness or injustice is free to admit his rage without appearing irrational or ungrateful. Therefore, human meanness is less harmful in its psychophysiological consequences than "goodness," even though both human goodness and human badness are expressions or consequences of a lower level of cognitive integration. They are manifestations of the calculating modes of being-in-the-world. Calculating man is double-minded, insincere, hypocritical and, above all, loveless.

Calculating man is incapable of loving. He is mainly concerned with the useful, the reasonable, the advantageous, the profitable, the right, the smart, the clever, the intelligent. For instance, one such "intelligent" parent—who always strove to be good and do the right thing—had the habit of kissing his child "affectionately" whenever he felt annoyed. His child became a severe behavior problem, with fits of rage and depressions. Calculating man is incapable of understanding because he tends to defile what he hears, sees, or reads by converting it to mere information and discursive knowledge. Often he impresses people as arrogant and tends to elicit unexplainable resentments. He cannot learn because he collects information. Intellectual man strives for mastery of the world and glory of the self.


## LOVING MAN

Loving man is concerned with understanding and responding, with illuminating, bearing witness to the truth. Loving man knows that only truth liberates, heals, and makes *"that all things work together for good"* (Rom. 8:28). Love does not calculate. Love is a supreme state of intelligence capable of understanding and seeing that which forever reveals itself. Love is that state of consciousness which brings man into harmony with what really is. Love is beyond good and evil. It comes into being through the modality of perception, called paying attention. Paying attention is related to Chuang-tzu's concept of "mind-fasting" and Jesus' recommendations of "prayer and fasting." Fasting implies a certain sacrifice, self-denial, or voluntary deprivation requisite for a higher level of intelligence to obtain in human consciousness and become manifest as wisdom and enlightened (inspired) understanding.

The term *paying attention* is, in itself, a semantic curiosity. One is led to ask: What is the payment in paying attention? The payment is like that in mind-fasting or in prayer and fasting: It is the giving up or sacrificing of certain mental content and of sensory and affective gratification. To pay attention, then, means that certain habits of thought—favored mental images, cherished assumptions—must be given up. Mental assumptions and affective gratifications constitute a "mental currency" to be paid for attainment of the loving mode of cognition.

The "open mind" is equally contingent on paying attention. Paying attention becomes the open-minded, loving-understanding approach to what is. It constitutes an epistemological principle upon which hinges the success of all psychotherapy, education, effective human communication, and, in the final analysis, health in general. For, as man is, so is his cognition; and as man's cognition is, so is he.

Loving man knows himself to be an expression of creative Intelligence, a transparency of Truth, an instrument of Understanding, a manifestation of Love, an *"image and likeness of God"* (Gen. 1:26). He sees life as an opportunity to become that which he truly is.

# Dialogue I

*Question:* You said just before you closed that love is beyond good and evil. I think it might be helpful if you perhaps amplified that, please.

*Dr. Hora:* Love entails a different mode of thought. The contemporary philosopher Heidegger has pointed out that there are two modes of thought. Accordingly, he distinguishes "das vorstellende Denken," which is the calculative mode of thought, and "das andenkende Denken," which is the loving, reverent, inspired thought. This has great significance for mental health, for the liberation of man's creative potentialities, and for the things mentioned previously.

*Question:* Are good and evil really relative, because if we become really loving, we don't have a controversy between good and evil?

*Dr. Hora:* We transcend them if we discover that we can think from the standpoint of love rather than from the standpoint of rationalism or utilitarianism. For the three modes of being-in-the-world that were described—the sensuous, the calculative and the intellectual—are a part of the human condition. Nevertheless, it is helpful to know that it's within the possibility of man to rise above them and reach that state of Existence where he can persistently endeavor to view life from the perspective of love rather than anything else.

*Question:* Then the common denominator is thought? Thought can be calculative or it can be loving, is that it? You said love is thought?

*Dr. Hora:* More correctly, love is a mode of cognition and response.

*Question:* It seems to me that I recognize all three in myself— that they exist together. The third condition I feel I have achieved only toward God or my conception of God, in which faith and

---

Dialogues I through VI are transcripts of discussions with the audience after delivery of the essays they follow—Ed.

love put all calculation and all rationality out of the picture. But I have never reached that state in regard to my fellow man—only in regard to the imperishable, intangible, metaphysical communion with God.

*Dr. Hora:* You fail to fulfill the commandment to love your neighbor? (laughter)

*Previous questioner:* Yes, I don't know how to achieve it but I feel it would be wonderful to achieve it. It does seem as if Jesus, for instance, and others who have achieved it in regard to their heavenly Spirit, or God, also had it toward man. I can't understand in myself just why such a cleavage is there.

*Dr. Hora:* Well, this is an important question. I hope that we will have a chance to go into it. The cleavage you refer to may have a lot to do with our ways of looking and seeing.

*Comment:* With humanity I analyze and separate and observe the faults and good points and see everybody from an intellectual perspective. But I never see God from an intellectual standpoint.

*Dr. Hora:* Right. This is the whole problem in a nutshell, namely, how can we outgrow psychological thinking? How can we rise above it? You point out the tremendous impact that psychology has on our consciousness. We are constantly picking out people's shortcomings.

*Comment:* They are so familiar.

*Dr. Hora:* There are many reasons for this. This certainly is the problem that prevents us from looking for love, seeing love and showing love.

*Comment:* But at least I feel that the partial achievement is the most precious thing in life to me by far. I would rather lose everything else than that. That is the most important thing in the world for happiness and for security, and so forth. And, with such extreme dependence and value put upon that, I often wonder why it doesn't seem to help me with the other.

*Question:* Isn't that one of the scary things in a passage from John, when John says that if you say you love God and hate your fellow man, you are a liar? (1 Jn. 4:20)

*Original questioner interrupts:* But I don't hate anybody! (laughter)

*Dr. Hora:* Now, let us try to consider this question. What is the meaning of the fact that we are more interested in people's weak points than in anything else? When we meet somebody, the first thing we notice is whether his hair is long, or whether he has a wart on his nose. Or does he have an accent? Is he crippled, etc.? The famous Swiss psychiatrist Ludwig Binswanger, who has made an original contribution to existential psychiatry, speaks of "Beim schwachen Punkte fassen," meaning that there is a tendency to grab people by their weak points, to focus attention on the other person's weakness.

*Question:*   Well, what does medical science do? Medicine is built on this.

*Dr. Hora:*   Doctors have a good excuse—they want to cure. (laughter) But what excuse do we have? (more laughter) No, I think that most of us are not sufficiently grounded on the rock of love. We seek security in a sense of superiority over our neighbor. If we can find some weakness in him, we feel stronger and safer.

*Question:*   It sounds neurotic.

*Dr. Hora:*   Of course.

*Question:*   Is that what James Baldwin has been trying to say to us?

*Dr. Hora:*   James Baldwin, the writer? I am not sufficiently familiar with his work but I wouldn't be surprised, for this is a very important point. However, black people are not exempt from this weakness either. This is a universal human problem, and the upsurge in popularity of psychoanalysis and psychology has reinforced this tendency. We must awaken to the realization that it is a weakness, not a strength. To be able to take people apart and discern in detail their weaknesses and their flaws in no way contributes to our sense of security. To learn to transcend this human tendency and to look for love and see love even if it is not apparent—this is the real source of assurance. I would say this is the work of righteousness of which Isaiah spoke: *"The work of righteousness shall be peace; and the effect of righteousness quietness and assurance for ever"* (Is. 32:17).

*Comment:*   Probably it is safe to say that while you were speaking, everyone was categorizing himself in one of the three classifications, and perhaps some of his friends as well. (laughter) I found myself categorizing Christ and the man you quoted as saying that the intellectual was interested in influencing the environment.

*Dr. Hora:*   Of course, from a certain standpoint it would seem that Jesus came to influence the world, but that influence was not manipulative: It was existential. He said, *"I am the way, the truth, and the life"* (Jn. 14:6). This is not personal influence. It is the influence of Truth that becomes manifest and is revealed through the life of man.

*Question:*   You said reality and love are beyond good and evil. But are they beyond destructive tendencies, destructive urges, and destructiveness itself? Don't you believe that man, even in a state of love, is always accessible to a destructive urge, to destructiveness, something in his nature that is destructive—the opposite of creativeness?

*Dr. Hora:*   If I understand correctly, the question is, Is man ever beyond evil? Or, can we ever rise above evil? (Questioner agrees). Destructiveness is a particular aspect of evil.

*Comment:*   If you were beyond evil, you could never be brought back to evil again, logically. If you were beyond it, it could not touch you. It is obvious we're not beyond it.

*Dr. Hora:*   But we didn't say that mortal man is beyond good and evil: We said love is. Even Mephisto, in Goethe's *Faust,* says, "I am the one that forever fosters evil and yet works for the cause of good." So you see, even the devil serves God, and of course this also points to the meaning of suffering. The meaning and purpose of suffering is to goad us to turn to that which is good.

*Question:*   Concerning cognitive integration, each level would be contained in the higher level, so there isn't any antagonism?

*Dr. Hora:*   Right.

*Comment:*   It is not a negation of these lower levels but an absorbing and transforming of them into another thing, not a negating of them—because they are part of our humanity.

*Question:*   I wonder if it wouldn't be helpful if we listed the different kinds of love. I doubt this is the kind you are speaking of.

*Dr. Hora:*   Right. We are talking about spiritual love, not carnal love or the love of gratification. What is ordinarily called love is not much more than appetite, whether it is in regard to a person of the opposite sex, or the same sex, or a sirloin steak, etc. Now, appetite has its place in life, sensory pleasures have their place in life, and so do intellectual and calculative thinking. These are important in business and industry and mathematics, in building a bridge, and so on. But we must not consider this as the ultimate of human attainment. We must rise higher, because Existence cannot be fulfilled just on that level.

# Illness and Health—
# What Are They?

The most primitive notion of illness is based on sensation. Since man's primordial conscious contact with the world seems to be mediated by the sensory apparatus, and since pain and pleasure are the basic features of sensory perception, pain has always been the basic element in man's conception of illness.

With the further development of human consciousness, man became cognizant of the significance of affective elements in his life experience, and thus he began to regard these as additional significant criteria of illness and health. This gave rise to a conception of illness based on disturbances of feelings, emotions, moods.

A third conception of illness is based on functioning. As man became a hunter, toolmaker, and builder of machines, he became keenly concerned with his capacities to perform the tasks he considered necessary for his survival and welfare. Furthermore, he learned to distinguish between physical functioning, mental-intellectual performance and social skills. Whenever man becomes hampered or incapable of performing some of his customary functions, he considers himself ill. The concern with bodily integrity as a basis for the conception of illness and health also belongs here.

Thus it appears that man's conception of health is inextricably tied up with his conception of illness. If he assumes that illness is pain, then he will seek health in painlessness or the opposite of pain, that is, pleasure. Here we encounter the term *disease,* which denotes a concept of illness based on the lack of ease. This often leads to a belief which holds that health is synonymous with ease. This in turn tends to give rise to therapeutic notions that view the pursuit of ease and pleasure as health-producing. There actually is a psychoanalytic theory that asserts that anhedonia, that is, "pleasure deficiency," is the etiological factor in schizophrenia.

Those who see the essence of illness in a disbalance of affectivity tend to seek health in the exploration and correction of these factors, which seem to be responsible for disturbances in feelings, emotions and moods. The central issue of health is here deemed to be rooted in the control of affectivity. Those who define illness in terms of disturbance of functions seek to find health in the re-establishment of these functions, be they sexual, physical, social-interpersonal, marital, occupational or otherwise.

However, all these conceptions of illness and health are but partial conceptions, even if taken all together in synthesis. For man is more than the sum total of his parts. As a matter of fact, he is something entirely different. There is no way of understanding what man is from the study of his parts. The objectification of man violates his essence and causes him to appear to be something else than what he truly is. It is the ontic perspective that would reveal him as he really is in the world. The importance of this lies in the fact that the proper view of man will lead to a better understanding of the conditions of his existence that comprise both illness and health. This view or perspective can be neither objective nor subjective nor purely psychological.

This is where the religious dimension makes its invaluable contribution by meeting with the existential viewpoint on the common ground of the ontic-ontological perspective. Both religion and existential psychiatry view man not as a complex apparatus that can break down in various areas, but as a being-in-the-world, that is, a spiritual being, an expression of God. To be capable of viewing man from an ontic perspective, the existential psychiatrist resorts to a mode of cognition that is neither sensory, nor affective, nor intellectual: It is phenomenological. Without a capacity for the phenomenological mode of cognition, existentialism is beyond the reach of the average scientifically trained individual. Moreover, it tends to strike some as an absurd and irritating nuisance. Therefore, some are inclined to dismiss it as mystical nonsense.

The philosophical discipline dedicated to the study of man as a being-in-the-world is called phenomenological ontology. Phenomenological ontology reveals that the essential characteristic of man as a being-in-the-world is that he sheds light on Existence, that is, he bears witness to it by manifesting it. He is a "clairiere de l' Existence," a "Lichtung des Daseins," as Heidegger puts it. He is capable of understanding and he can help understanding.

He is able to know and to know that he knows: he is able to transmit knowledge. His mental horizon reaches far beyond sensory perception, instinct gratification, intellection. He is a presence in this world and through his presence truth and love can become manifest.

When man is in harmony with Existence he is in "at-one-ment" with it, unseparated. He is whole, he is healthy, well, authentic. He is a medium of goodness, intelligence, creativity and love. The qualities of the Transcendent shine through his being. His presence in the world is a beneficial one. When a man is in disharmony with Existence, he is separated from the ground of his being. He is apart, he is partial, he is not whole, not holy, not well, he is ill. The existential viewpoint on illness and health is also to be found in the root meanings of the words: illness = evilness, healthiness = wholeness. Just as evil is the absence of good (boni, as defined by St. Augustine), illness is the absence of wholeness.

In existential psychiatric terms man is ill when his existence is misdirected and fragmented. He is healed when he returns to a mode of being-in-the-world that brings him into "at-one-ment," that is, harmony with his essential individual existentiality.

From an epistemological standpoint the issues of illness and health revolve around the peculiar characteristic of human consciousness: On the one hand, it is capable of being fragmented by misdirected concerns, in which case man may manifest a variety of discordant phenomena, which we call pathology; or, on the other hand, it can reach its optimum cognitive and creative potentialities by awakening to the loving mode of being-in-the-world, which we call wholesome, healthy, authentic existence.

# The Transpersonal Perspective

When attempting to convey something of the nature of existential psychotherapy, one usually encounters some difficulties of a conceptual, semantic, philosophical and epistemological nature. Perhaps the greatest difficulty arises, however, from the fact that the existential psychotherapist is required to meet his patient on a different ground, that is, he must utilize a different mode of cognition and view his patient from a different perspective than is customary in the natural sciences or in much of everyday life.

Under ordinary circumstances man is generally inclined to view the world around him either from a subjective or an objective standpoint, or from an intellectual-analytic-interpretative standpoint. The subjectivist is concerned with the question "How do I feel about it?"; the objectivist asks "What is it?"; and the intellectual-analytic interpreter asks "Why is it?" or "What is it for?" The subjectivist is inevitably egotistical; he is involved with his own feelings and sensations, which he calls personal experiences. The objectivist tends to be reifying and materialistic; he considers himself rational, logical, objective, and scientific. The intellectual is inquisitive and knowledgeable; he relies on theories, frames of reference, and ideologies; he is an adherent of schools of thought. More often than not, however, these three modes of relating are intermixed in the same individual, with one or the other mode taking precedence. To illustrate, let us take an example from psychotherapeutic practice. A middle-aged man comes for help for obesity, a lifelong problem that has yielded neither to somatic nor to psychoanalytic therapies. The phenomenological analysis of his mode of being-in-the-world reveals a disguised concern with being a "big man," towering over others physically, mentally, and emotionally in order to be "immovable." He seeks a situation of unassailable security and advantage in life, and he has succeeded in shaping himself into a Goliath.

19

The subjectively responding therapist might point out that the patient makes him feel small and helpless. The patient in turn probably would say to himself, "I'm glad to hear that. That makes me feel good." The objective therapist might concern himself with the patient's nutrition and eating habits. He might even recommend a diet and drugs. The danger here is that should the patient be induced to lose weight, he may feel robbed of his power, security or greatness; and it is conceivable that as a consequence he could develop a depressive reaction or a compensatory megalomaniacal psychosis.

It is, therefore, very important that a patient be helped to lose the meaning of his disease before he loses the symptom. This may very well throw light on the perennial problem of side effects and secondary complications following therapeutic interventions and treatment procedures where patients were treated as objects.

The analytical therapist would be inclined to make psychodynamic interpretations on the basis of historical-causal-genetic explorations. However, causality and meaning are not identical, and causal-genetic interpretations seldom have therapeutic value because cause-and-effect thinking is too shallow and narrowly circumscribed. It fails to comprehend existence as a meaningful and meaning-orientated process. Furthermore, seeking reasons and causes only results in finding excuses that tend to impede therapeutic progress rather than to enhance it. As the French put it, *On ne guerit pas en se souvenant, mais on se souvient en guerissant* (One does not heal by remembering, but one remembers as a result of healing).

From an existential standpoint, problems and discordant conditions are consequences of misdirected concerns. Therefore, strictly speaking, problems cannot be solved. The endeavor to solve problems is a misdirected concern in itself and tends to compound the initial problem. Thus, when people try to iron out their difficulties by discussing them at length, they paradoxically get more and more embroiled in conflict. Debates and dialectics tend to compound problems rather than to solve them. Nor is it wise, however, to ignore problems, withdraw from them or avoid facing up to them. Problems are resolved when misdirected concerns are corrected by being lost; but to be lost, they first must be found, that is, phenomenologically perceived and elucidated. Only after they are thus found can they be lost.

False concerns are lost when attention is shifted toward more wholesome concerns. When false concerns vanish from consciousness, that is, lose their personal significance, they cease to generate problems, complications and existential crises. Wholesome concerns—a basic element of which is a transpersonal perspective—lead to wholesome attitudes, and these in turn result in harmonious life experiences and mental health. In the case cited, for instance, the existential approach would be neither subjective, nor objective, nor analytical—it would be transpersonal. The existential therapist would endeavor to discern the meaning and character of the patient's mode of being-in-the-world as it is revealed in the psychotherapeutic encounter. When the meaning of a symptom is phenomenologically elucidated, the patient discovers that his suffering is a consequence of misdirected concerns and erroneous assumptions about existence; he then becomes vitally interested in finding more wholesome concerns.

The general validity and significance of the transpersonal perspective can be illustrated further by considering the issue of parental attitudes. For example, should a father's attitude toward his daughter be a predominantly subjective one, he would reveal a concern with how his own feelings were stimulated by his daughter. This could take on a variety of meanings, from mildly egocentric to overtly incestuous and seductive. Should the father's attitude be an objective one, he might reduce his daughter to a "thing" by objectifying her, perhaps causing her to lose her sense of human worth. Finally, should the father be intellectually inclined and analytically minded, he might generate a great deal of anxiety, indecision and confusion by interpreting causal connections and motivations. The psychologizing perspective can engender a variety of tendencies, from exaggerated intellectual self-preoccupations to self-conscious inhibition, from loss of spontaneity to, conceivably, catatonic rigidity or paranoid delusions.

The subjectivist parent tends to bring up selfish, hypochondriacal, sexually overstimulated and hedonistic children. The objectivist parent often appears tyrannical and his children tend to become recalcitrant and rebellious, while the analytical and psychologizing parent may well be a source of schizophrenic reactions in his family. It is the loving parent who understands, for his concern is with truth and beneficence.

More often than not, man is quite confused about how to respond to life situations. He may attempt intermittently to be subjective, relying on his feelings and sensations; or objective, relying on his sensory perceptions; or analytical, relying on his preconceptions. Indeed, ordinarily unenlightened man seems to have a choice between these three erroneous modes of responding. This choice tends to create confusion, a tendency to unintentional hypocrisy. This is a serious professional hazard often afflicting those in the social sciences as well as so-called cured patients. It may be described as a predilection toward saying that one feels something, when actually one only thinks it or knows about it from books or lectures. For instance, it is not unusual to hear someone say, "I feel that this man has an Oedipus complex" or "I feel that this patient relates himself to his wife on an anal-sadistic level." Such involuntary hypocrisy indicates a failure to differentiate between what one knows and what one thinks, what one observes and what one feels. Yet, personal integrity and clarity of communication are fundamental, and must be of primary concern to all who would endeavor to foster mental health.

Another manifestation of unintended hypocrisy is the tendency to pretend interest while pursuing inquisitiveness. At first glance, the difference seems very slight, yet neglecting a clear differentiation can have far-reaching consequences. To be interested is to love and revere; to be inquisitive, however, is to intrude, trespass, violate. This subtle difference constitutes the essence of the existential attitude, which is called "letting be" and which allows the therapeutic process to proceed with a minimum of the so-called resistance phenomenon.

It is important, therefore, to realize that all three modes of cognition—subjective, objective, analytical—are in a sense pathogenic and inaccurate. Furthermore, the indiscriminate mixing of the three is incompatible with clear communication and harmonious living.

It is essential to discover a mode of cognition that is not subjective, objective, or analytical. This can be attained through the transpersonal perspective. The existential psychotherapist is not a participant observer, a nonparticipant interpreter, an empathizer or a sympathizer—he is an understander. He is a *clairiere de l' Existence,* one who sheds light on Existence. His is a perspective of love. Love here means a mode of being-in-the-world and a mode of cognition. Love, as a mode of cognition, is concerned with truth, with meaning, and with the unhindered unfolding of human potentialities. A loving man is concerned with participating in existence as a beneficial presence. Such love is not personal, interpersonal, or impersonal. It is transpersonal.

Wholesome human existence and mental health are here understood to be contingent on an epistemological principle that makes it possible for man to transcend his tendency toward calculative thinking, "das vorstellende Denken," and become available to creative, inspired modes of thought, "das andenkende Denken." The capacity to view the patient from a transpersonal perspective is basic to existential psychotherapy.

# Dialogue II

*Question:* By diseases, do we mean diseases in general, including degenerative, cancerous, malignant, inherited and so forth— or just mental disease?
*Audience:* All.
*Question:* Then how is cancer expressed existentially?
*Dr. Hora:* As noted, diseases as well as human problems, discordant conditions of life are understood to be the fruits of misdirected modes of being-in-the-world. At this stage, not all forms of misdirected modes of being-in-the-world can be sufficiently discerned and elucidated. We all live, more or less, the wrong way and therefore bear wrong fruit accordingly. Still, a large number of diseases and discordant conditions yield quite readily the moment their proper meaning is discerned to be a consequence of a particular form of misdirected mode of being-in-the-world, that is, an erroneous orientation in life. When this is specifically clarified and corrected, the consequences tend to disappear. For example, it is quite evident that problems per se cannot be solved. Whenever we are confronted with a problem, we try to solve the problem itself directly, and the harder we try to do this, the more complicated it tends to become. Sometimes we deceive ourselves that we do solve our problems, but if we do, we generate others. Problems are consequences of false concerns and only by correcting these false concerns, or errors in living, whether minor or major, do problems resolve themselves.
*Question:* Do we have to face them at least?
*Dr. Hora:* Oh, yes.
*Question:* I mean, get as clear a view of the problem as possible?
*Dr. Hora:* We have to see beyond the problem.
*Question:* In the attainment of a oneness with Existence that you spoke about as essential to health, is each oneness a different oneness for each individual? Is there a general level that operates for everybody?
*Dr. Hora:* Everyone is unique and yet everyone is the image and likeness of the same God.

*Question:* But everyone comes equipped differently to face Existence with what he's equipped with?

*Dr. Hora:* The unique endowment of every individual has the optimum possibility of unfoldment under one condition that is common to all mankind, namely, being in harmony with the Fundamental Order of Being.

*Question:* I'd like to come back to the question, How helpful would it be to be attuned to Existence for someone who has a malignant illness? Does not the physical fact remain?

*Comment:* I can answer that. I have a malignancy for which I had surgery. It was secondary, which means there is a primary source someplace and it just doesn't make any difference. It just isn't important.

*Dr. Hora:* Malignancy is not incurable. I will put it this way: What seems incurable may yet be healable.

*Comment:* Even if it isn't, it just doesn't matter that much.

*Dr. Hora:* But it matters that it be healed.

*Question:* On a physical basis?

*Dr. Hora:* On a total basis. Man is not just a physical being.

*Question:* Doesn't some confusion result in the fact that most people equate disease and health with good and evil?

*Dr. Hora:* Yes, of course. People who are inclined to be moralistic might tend to assume a judgmental attitude implicitly.

*Question:* There's a very simple illustration of a person who wears glasses: evidently a disease is there or he wouldn't need to wear glasses. If he had never used his eyes, he would never have needed to wear glasses, and then he would be uneducated, a simpleton.

*Dr. Hora:* If he had never used his eyes, chances are he would be blind. But of course, we must not become moralistic about illness; we must have a broad view of the human condition. It is important to face up to the fact that the human condition is such that man's ignorance is constantly destroying him. So we could say that illness and suffering are unnecessary yet inevitable, because we still haven't reached the point of knowing how to live in harmony with God.

*Question:* Well then, Jesus didn't live in harmony with God.

*Dr. Hora:* Was he sick?

*Comment:* He could have escaped it, I suppose, if he'd acted differently, but he thought his suffering was an inevitable part of his being, perhaps to carry his message to us.

*Dr. Hora:* Without going deeper into the theological implications of the crucifixion, perhaps this might be relevant. During our worship meeting today a thought kept recurring, namely, that without distractions we could not be conscious of union with God. Therefore, we can learn to appreciate the value of distractions. If there were no distractions in life we would not be able to be conscious of God and of the possibility of at-one-ment with him. Since man is conscious, he must seek the solutions to life consciously. What is the meaning of the word *distractions?* To distract means to draw away—we are being drawn away. From what? From harmony, peace, love. We could say that the devil has a function. It is good to know this, because if we don't know it we get involved with fighting the devil, and if we fight the devil we embrace him. If, for instance, you try to meditate and someone sitting near you is fidgeting, making notes, and jabbing you with his elbow, what do you do? If you get involved with it, if you resent it, then of course you are lost. If you try to escape it, then you are involved with it. If you try to excuse it and be nice about it, you are also involved with it. So what do you do?

*Comment:*   You ignore it.

*Dr. Hora:*   If you try to ignore it, you are involved with it.

*Comment:*   I would discuss it with the person.

*Dr. Hora:*   Then you would be involved with it. If you are involved with the distraction, then you are completely distracted.

*Comment:*   Endeavor to get deeper into meditation so as to become lost to sensation and to these thoughts. Try to transcend it in the depth of your unity—you have to reach a higher level—or try to look upon it as a spur to help you reach your goal.

*Dr. Hora:*   That's right. You are absolutely correct. It is a spur. Has everybody heard this? Would you say it loudly?

*Comment:*   I think you can look upon many kinds of distractions in the world as blessings in disguise and spurs to move you in the opposite direction—in the direction to which you really ought to go and not be distracted.

*Dr. Hora:*   As you see, this example refers to our entire life, because all sorts of distractions are constantly interfering with our consciousness of harmony and love.

*Question:*   Is there a place in all this for the feeling that there was a time when we were so much a part of this—and we were completely unaware of it—and then something happened so that we had to struggle back? Is this the meaning and goal of life?

*Dr. Hora:* The basic issue is epistemological. If we were not subject to distractions, then we would be in harmony with God—but we would never know it. If we understand this, then this throws a different light on the problem of distractions. We do not have to resent them, nor do we have to like them, but by understanding their inevitability and function we can transcend them. We can only transcend that which we understand from an existential standpoint. What we don't understand we cannot transcend because we get involved with it mentally, emotionally and physically.

*Question:* If disease is a disturbance of the at-one-ment with God, wouldn't you expect a great increase in diseases in an atheistic society?

*Dr. Hora:* Is there such a thing as an atheistic society?

*Comment:* I feel a person can be religious and at the same time a philosophical atheist.

*Dr. Hora:* There are no atheistic societies; there are only atheistic ideologies. The individual is forever reaching out for God, whether he knows it, or admits it. Man's troubles come from reaching out for God in wrong directions.

*Questions:* How do we arrive at the at-one-ment with God?

*Dr. Hora:* As was pointed out, neither subjectively, nor objectively, nor analytically, but through the endeavor to persist in the loving outlook on life regardless of the aggressiveness of distractions.

*Question:* Doesn't the existential psychiatrist use anything of the analytical and intellectual approach in analysis?

*Dr. Hora:* There are various brands of existentialism.

*Question:* This is rather a high concept of philosophy or religion—but if one has a patient who is stuck in a materialistic imbalance, is there not necessarily a time when he has to unravel and look at things causally and analytically in order to just unload a little?

*Dr. Hora:* People often insist on it.

*Question:* I'd like to try to restate the same question. If understanding is important or necessary to transcendence, then isn't there a place for depth psychology?

*Dr. Hora:* Depth psychology is very interesting and there is a place for it in the study and exploration of the human psyche, but for healing there is only "height psychology."

*Question:* Isn't transpersonal love sufficient without God? Why is it necessary to bring in God? That's where the atheistic question comes in, doesn't it? Why God, which has been carried through the centuries in so many distorted ways? Why God?

*Dr. Hora:* Transpersonal Love—if you capitalize it—becomes a synonym for God. You can call God many names, but the important thing is to understand God as Love, or Love-Intelligence, or Cosmic Consciousness, or Creative Force. But just as you can use many names for the right God, you can use the word *God* for many erroneous concepts of God. As long as we understand correctly, that's all that matters. This also answers the question about atheistic societies. As you know, in an unguarded moment even Khrushchev mentioned the name of God.

*Question:* What is Existence? You use the words *Existence* and *existential* in a way I really don't understand.

*Dr. Hora:* Existential is that which concerns life; Existence is the manifestation of the Reality that constitutes life, which man reveals. That's why Existence can also be considered a synonym for God. If we say that man manifests Existence, it amounts to saying that man is the image and likeness of God. Now, the reason this is a mystery is because Existence as God, as Love, is neither concrete nor abstract. That which is neither concrete nor abstract defies thought.

*Comment:* This is the nonthinkable you mentioned.

*Dr. Hora:* Right. That which is concrete is tangible, that which is abstract is thinkable, but that which is neither tangible nor thinkable stumps us. We are up against a wall. Our conceptual possibilities are exhausted, yet our cognitive possibilities are not exhausted.

*Comment:* Something in us says it is so.

*Dr. Hora:* We cannot think it, but we can discern its presence.

*Question:* I am concerned about disease—dis-ease, pain, illness, suffering—since we have known beautiful souls whose lives have been full of suffering and yet have seemed more beautiful because of it or through it. I don't quite see how we can say that these things are a misdirection. Is it possible that they could be, in a sense, a gift given us in order to goad us to further progress?

*Dr. Hora:* Yes, but it is hard to conceive of God giving such gifts, you know, because God is Love.

*Comment:* Jesus said this himself in answer to the man who was blind. He was asked, *"Who did sin, this man, or his parents?"*

And the answer was, "*Neither—but that the works of God should be made manifest in him*" (Jn. 9:2-3).

*Dr. Hora:*   That's right, but not by the blindness.

*Question:*   By what, then?

*Dr. Hora:*   By the healing of it. God is glorified by healing, by that which is good. That which is evil needs to be overcome. The purpose of evil and suffering is that they may be overcome.

*Comment:*   The Bible speaks of God as He "*who healeth all thy diseases*" (Ps. 103:3).

*Dr. Hora:*   That's right.

*Question:*   There is no other agency in healing?

*Dr. Hora:*   I don't think so.

*Question:*   Is there Existence without man?

*Dr. Hora:*   If the question is asked, Is there Existence without man?, we could also ask, Is there God without man? And how can we be sure?

*Comment:*   Jesus said, "*Before Abraham was, I am*" (Jn. 8:58).

*Dr. Hora:*   Yes.

*Comment:*   That is the consciousness of life without beginning or end—no relation to materialization at all.

*Dr. Hora:*   God is revealed through man. When they were saying to Jesus, "*Show us the Father and it sufficeth us,*" he said, "*He that hath seen me hath seen the Father*" (Jn. 14:8-9). If we look at each other we can see God, provided we know how to look.

*Question:*   We have been talking about using distractions as spurs to further growth toward God. It takes a good deal of effort to achieve this overcoming of distractions. Some psychiatric patients seem to lack the will to make the effort to overcome them. I am wondering how (and I think all of us are perhaps guilty of this to a certain extent) the fat man who is enjoying his food can be helped to make the effort to overcome difficulties.

*Dr. Hora:*   The purpose of suffering is to motivate us toward salvation and healing. We cannot do it; we cannot motivate someone. Salvation cannot be sold. It must be available.

# Beyond Self

When the ancient Chinese scholar Yen Hui was considering becoming court adviser to the ill-famed ruler of his time, he came to his teacher, Chuang-tzu, for advice. Chuang-tzu warned him that he was in great danger of being beheaded unless he learned "mind-fasting." Heedful of this advise, Yen Hui retired to practice mind-fasting in accordance with his teacher's instructions.

Three years later, Yen Hui returned to his teacher saying he was ready for his assignment. The master challenged him to prove it, whereupon Yen Hui said: "Before I disciplined myself in mind-fasting, as you instructed me, I was fully conscious of being Yen Hui. Now that I have perfected myself in the discipline, I realize that from the beginning there never was a Yen Hui." The master said: "Yes, you realized *hsu* [Emptiness]."

Voodoo is a primitive tribal method of inflicting illness, suffering and, on occasion, even death upon a condemned individual. This is accomplished by sticking pins into an effigy doll. The amazing effects of this method demonstrate the vulnerability of man, in whose consciousness the body, as the "I am," represents primary reality. In the consciousness of the victim, the voodoo doll becomes an extension and a representative of the self, and whatever happens to this image is experienced by the victim personally and directly. In other words, the abstract ideas portrayed by the effigy are concretized in the somatic sphere of the victim, to such an extent that medical science has in some instances been helpless in counteracting the "spell." The voodoo spell is then a suggestive system whereby the abstract may become demonstrably concretized in the form both of experiences and of bodily changes. Thought, as word and image, becomes experience, as feeling and flesh. Voodoo is effective as long as there is a shared

31

belief in the reality of assumed notions. The voodoo doll is the shared symbol of the victim's self.

Symbols are representations of man's notions about Reality. Symbols are the products of man's desire to give form to that which forever must remain formless. *"I AM THAT I AM,"* said God to Moses (Ex. 3:14), which means, "I am that which forever is," or "I am that which really is." In human consciousness, the body tends to be a symbol of the self. Body sensations thus become symbolic thoughts (dreams) about reality of the self.

Human thinking is prevalently dedicated to proving the reality of one important basic assumption, namely, that man exists as a separate and self-sustaining entity in time and space. In other words, human thinking is prevalently preoccupied with self-confirmation. This type of thinking is always circular, and it circles around its own hypothetical center.

Bodily sensations tend to reveal in symbolic fashion self-confirmatory desires. The body becomes the symbolic manifestation of thought mistaking itself for reality. In other words, the body reveals man's inclination to view reality from that center which calls itself the self. One might ask: What is that center around which the self-centered man is centered? Where is this center located? What does it consist of? And how does it come into being?

The self is a conceptual center of being, built up from accumulated assumptions about the nature of reality, as mediated by man's sensory apparatus and discursive thought. *Nihil est in intellectu quod primum non fuerit in sensu* (The intellect knows only that which has come through the senses). The self is then built up from what appears to be and what should be. Moreover, what "should be" insists on ignoring what really is.

Concepts are statements about reality. They have no reality of their own, and their location is in that unknown place called memory and mind. Thus the self, or the "I am," cannot be localized nor does it have reality of its own. Yet ordinary man spends most of his life in an unceasing effort to confirm this abstraction as a concrete reality. The need to confirm the reality of the self is in itself evidence of a lurking doubt existing in man's awareness.

It is this disquieting, lurking doubt that underlies the ubiquitous human inclination toward self-assertiveness. When self-assertive man becomes aware of the suffering he brings upon himself and others, he tries to behave in self-restraining or self-effacing ways. However, self-restraint is but the assertion of the self against itself.

Therefore, it leads only to further suffering. For both self-assertiveness and self-restraint are ignoring what really is by being preoccupied with what "should be." Ignorance is that mental activity that ignores what really is.

In contemplating human existence and social life as an endless scramble and struggle with the problems of self-confirmation, one is faced with a fountain of despair, conflict and suffering. The significance of childhood experiences and cultural trends lies to a great extent in the fact that they provide people with particular patterns of self-confirmatory strivings.

The tragic element of the human condition is rooted in that cognitive deficiency which underlies the desire of man to confirm his self as reality. Since the self is that which "should be," it is not possible to confirm it constructively, for only the confirming of what really is can be constructive. The effort at confirming what "should be" is therefore destructive of reality. Consequently, it is pathogenic. Disease is that shadow which the "I am" casts upon Existence. For the "I am" to be reality, the world must be destroyed. The acute psychotic experience of world destruction is the birth of the delusion concerning an autonomous, exclusive "I am."

One young man teetering on the brink of a psychotic break was so involved in self-confirmatory preoccupations in the form of grandiose boasting that, when he tried not to boast, he became plagued with painful erections. When he came to understand the erections as vicarious boasting on the sexual plane, he lost them, but he began to feel cramps in his lower extremities. When he understood them as yet another way of the body's saying "I am," they also left him. At this point, he began to feel a need to tighten his shoelaces repeatedly to keep himself "together," that is, to feel himself as a self.

Suffering is the consequence of that cognitive deficiency in man which gives rise to self-confirmatory desires. Self-confirmatory strivings keep him in a state of ignorance by inducing him to ignore that which really is. Physical suffering is the body in the process of confirming itself. The "body-mind" speaks directly prior to verbal language. Language is one step removed from the event of self-confirmation taking place in the organism.

As long as artistic expression is self-confirmatory in nature, it is not truly creative and has little integrative value. True art expresses Reality, which does not mean that it is necessarily realistic in the conventional sense of the word. True art illumines the hitherto unseen; art broadens man's consciousness and cognition. It is therefore integrative both for the artist and for the observer. Creativity has its meaning in illuminating man's relationship to his ontological Ground. The creative artist helps man to see and worship.

The progressive dissolution of the subject in modern painting can be understood as the present-day expression of the perennial search for intuitive cognition of Reality. Modern art is thus a record of the artist's cognition of Reality. Art is at once a medium of cognition, of documentation, and of communication of the artist's quest for Ultimate Reality. As man is, so is his cognition. As a true artist creates, so is he. The true artist and his creation are one. By searching for Reality, the artist is ultimately seeking his own place in it. As a man's cognition is, so is he.

It is interesting to note the essentially opposing directions that characterize modern art and mental disease. Both modern art and mental disease are manifestations of man's struggle for Reality. Mental disease wants to clutch at the object world, even at the price of concretizing the abstract, that is, objectifying thought. Modern art moves in the direction of abstracting and dissolving the concrete object beyond thought into pure experience. The mentally sick want to lean on sensory perception as a foundation for contact with Reality. The modern artist seeks to go beyond the senses toward the intuitive transcending-loving mode of cognition of Reality.

We could say that the mentally sick are aware of the nonobjective world and are threatened by it, whereas the healthy artist enters it by free choice and is able to return from it unscathed, even enriched in his being. The mentally sick live in dread of nothingness and strive to escape from it; the healthy artist seeks to embrace it and to know it reverently.

When man becomes aware of the suffering inherent in idolatry of the self, or of the other, or of what "seems to be" and what "should be," he discovers that "self-realization" is an altogether misleading idea, both in art and in psychiatry. Health is contingent not on self-realization but on realization of Reality.

Selfishness, indifference, and inconsiderateness are consequences of insufficient cognition prevailing in common man. Self-centered man calculates, plots, and schemes his own self-confirmation. In the process he unfailingly harms himself and others.

Most human suffering reveals the presence of self-centeredness and calculative thinking. If the self is thus revealed as unreal and empty, the question arises as to what is really Real?

If all that is unreal is essentially sensory and conceptual, then true Reality must be that which is beyond the sensory and conceptual, which means that there must be a mode of consciousness that transcends the sensory and the conceptual. It must be, then, supra-sensory and transcending. Man awakens to its realization in proportion to his understanding of the limitations of the sensory and conceptual spheres of preoccupation. At this point, self-consciousness yields to transcending consciousness.

Enlightened man transcends his self in "seeing the truth of what is." In this process of losing himself, he finds that which is Real. He heals, that is, he becomes whole (holy) in his "at-one-ment" with Reality. The seer becomes the seeing, and the seeing becomes the seen. Love is thus re-cognized (rediscovered) to be a mode of cognition. Love is found to be that intelligence which forever reveals itself as Understanding.

In the experience of understanding, the true nature of Reality is revealed. In it there is neither "self" nor "other"; there is only the all-transcending, timeless process manifesting itself in that "field of phenomena" of which man is the medium *(L'homme clairiere de l' Existence)*.

Self-centered consciousness does not discern the Ground of Being. Interpersonal consciousness is focused on the interaction of the self and the other; it fails to see that background without which the foreground could not appear. The interpersonal focus ignores the truth of what really is, because it is concerned with the relationship of the self to the other. It does not realize that the self is the same as the other, since the other is but another self. In the realm of understanding, there is neither "self " nor "other"; there is only that which really is. Love is self-less. It is that background of harmony which is obscured, but also revealed, by the foreground of the discordant self.

# Dialogue III

*Question:* If Yen Hui had attained "Emptiness," why did he want the position?

*Dr. Hora:* To benefit the people, to protect the people from the ruthless emperor.

*Question:* What about Jesus antagonizing the Pharisees?

*Dr. Hora:* Well, what about it?

*Question:* Well, you said that this Yen Hui fellow would probably not antagonize or provoke anybody.

*Comment:* I don't think Jesus did antagonize. The antagonism was from the Pharisees, first of all.

*Dr. Hora:* Undoubtedly, Jesus meant to be beneficial by antagonizing the Pharisees, but it would not have been beneficial for Yen Hui to antagonize or arouse some brutal impulses in the emperor. The criterion is to be able to participate in Existence as a beneficial presence; in order to be able to live that way, personal considerations must not stand in the way. And that is quite an attainment.

*Comment:* I just thought that this was analogous to being a catalytic agent on a human level.

*Dr. Hora:* You could say it that way. A beneficial agent. Yes. A Bodhisattva. A beneficial presence rather than a personality.

*Question:* What is the motivation for getting into this difficult state of mind of being a beneficial presence? Why should anyone want to do it?

*Dr. Hora:* This constitutes the ultimate good.

*Question:* Could you say that this is a Zen motive?

*Dr. Hora:* You could say that, yes. Does anybody know what's good about being good? (laughter)

*Comment:* It's not bad (more laughter).

*Comment:* It makes you feel better.

*Dr. Hora:* It makes you feel better?

*Comment:* . . . when you are good.

*Dr. Hora:* Feeling better would not be sufficient reason. Apparently human existence cannot reach its optimum fulfillment any other way.

36

*Question:*   Isn't it a little dangerous to use those "good" and "bad" terms? Aren't you getting into the "ought" realm right away, which is a part of this concrete fiction?

*Dr. Hora:*   The "ought" realm, in this case, is determined by God, not by man. The self or the "should" is determined by human imagination and environmental expectations. That is the difference.

*Question:*   How do we know that?

*Comment:*   Well, isn't there just a feeling—I don't know how to put it positively, but negatively—a feeling of tremendous dissatisfaction because we feel that we are not realizing the potential that is pulling us beyond ourselves?

*Dr. Hora:*   Yes, you are hinting at what is called by some people existential frustration.

*Question:*   What is existential frustration?

*Dr. Hora:*   When the potentialities inherent in us are not given a chance to unfold and to come to fruition, we experience existential frustration.

*Question:*   You said that Love is that Intelligence which reveals understanding.

*Dr. Hora:*   Which reveals itself as Understanding.

*Question:*   Then is there feeling in this concept of love, or is it intelligence?

*Dr. Hora:*   The prevailing view of love is that it is an emotion, a feeling—and this is how we jump to the conclusion that the opposite of love is hate. Conversely, if we think the opposite of love is hate, then we assume that love is a feeling. Now, love does not exclude feelings. Feelings are concomitant experiences in love, but they do not constitute love. The opposite of love is scheming, that is, calculative thinking.

*Question:*   What then is compassion?

*Dr. Hora:*   Compassion, I would say, is a modality of love directed toward another living creature. But love does not have to be directed toward anybody in particular because love is much more than just a relationship between people. Love transcends people. After all, Love is God.

*Question:*   Can we go back to Yen Hui? I am still a little puzzled. If he really had this experience—realizing the self that led him into this wisdom that wouldn't arouse anger—wouldn't it also take away his fear of death?

*Dr. Hora:*   No doubt.

*Question:*   He was safe on more than one level?

*Dr. Hora:*   Certainly, but he would be of no use dead. He wanted to be beneficial. It says in the texts of Taoism that the people were heavily oppressed at that time and he wanted to help them.

*Question:*   Would this state of emptiness that Yen Hui achieved also relieve him of suffering?

*Dr. Hora:*   I should think so.

*Question:*   Then might not this be the real goal?

*Dr. Hora:*   Escape from suffering? It's quite a valid motivation.

*Question:*   But isn't that a self-centered motivation?

*Dr. Hora:*   Yes, it is, except that as long as it is just that, it does not succeed.

*Question:*   Suppose you have a patient who rather enjoys his suffering because it makes him know he is alive. He doesn't want to give it up, even though it is pretty intense. How can you generate a goal, a vision, of what he might be? Can you, as a therapist, help him do that?

*Dr. Hora:*   It is doubtful.

*Question:*   You said you were going to tell us phenomenologically how to do it. (laughter)

*Dr. Hora:*   I was going to tell you what phenomenological elucidation means.

*Question:*   What does it mean?

*Dr. Hora:*   Without a patient's desire for healing, little can be done. Suffering reaches a point, of course, when man wants to be liberated. He can change his mind again. There was a gentle man who paid people to beat him. He liked it, but suffered too. He was rather undecided about a cure. Nothing could be done for him until the time he was completely fed up with it. We can take a horse to water but we can't make him drink.

*Question:*   Well, this is what makes me wonder why the sensuous man was in the therapeutic hour—the man who ate words and after the hour expelled them? Why would he even be in a psychotherapeutic hour if this was all he was doing with it? Was he looking seriously for help?

*Dr. Hora:*   Yes, he thought he wanted help. He had various difficulties in life, which of course he would have like to gotten rid of, but in the process of seeking help he went about it the wrong way. He had the wrong attitude toward help. He had to be shown that it was not possible for him to be liberated from his complications as long as his attitude to life was an alimentary one, and as long as he was just eating everything and digesting it and getting rid of it. So his attitude had to change; it was up to him whether he was willing or not. If someone is reluctant at one time, he may be amenable at another time.

*Question:* Would you say that all suffering that we endure— whatever the form may be—is due to disobedience of the Reality within, to disobedience to God? If we are truly obedient, there would be no suffering?

*Dr. Hora:* If we were obedient, there would be no suffering?

*Question:* Obedient to God's will.

*Dr. Hora:* Yes, but we don't know quite how to be obedient. We are rather ignorant.

*Question:* But if we could attain it, would it negate suffering?

*Dr. Hora:* Undoubtedly.

*Question:* Buber spoke of a singer who learned to sing to God. Wasn't he being obedient?

*Dr. Hora:* Yes, he discovered that it is no use trying to sing to people. Here is a very important point; namely, we have accepted the idea that if man learns how to deal with his fellow man he will be healthy. Does this really work?

*Comment:* Not today, it doesn't.

*Dr. Hora:* It doesn't work because it leaves God out of the picture. It is therefore not in harmony with reality. It is an unrealistic expectation. One cannot become healthy by knowing how to get along with people. One can only learn to be a skillful manipulator of human relationships. But that has nothing to do with being healthy. There are psychopaths who get along very well with people.

*Question:* Would you say that Jesus suffered more or less preparatory to the crucifixion? Would you say his suffering increased or decreased? Do you think, as he grew into awareness of his Father, his suffering would have decreased?

*Dr. Hora:* These are very hard questions. Once I had a conversation with a Zen master about Jesus, and he, not knowing how to express himself in English, drew a picture of him carrying the cross smiling. This is their concept of the crucifixion, and apparently they can prove it, too. Look at what is happening in South Vietnam: These people can burn themselves alive. Apparently they have a mastery of pain that is beyond our understanding.

*Question:* Is there an understanding of the purpose of pain? In a book I am reading, there is an example of a man who lost his wife and was very much disturbed. When he sought help, he was asked: If his wife were spared, how would she feel in his place? He conceded she would be in great pain and discomfort. It was explained that she was then relieved of the pain and that his burden was the pain. He was told, "You are paying the price of her liberation through your pain." He was relieved because he then understood why he had the pain.

*Dr. Hora:* This is from Dr. Frankl's work. It sounds somewhat like rationalizing away grief. Some people can probably do this. Some people have strong powers of rationalization, but I don't think that this is the best answer to the problem of grief.

*Comment:* Grief is self-pity. He was pitying himself. His grief was really for himself, for his own deprivation.

*Dr. Hora:* There are different approaches to the problem of grief. Certainly grief is a very serious pain. These are palliative methods. "Palliative" means pain-relieving psychotherapeutic interventions, which have no part in man's broader realization of Existence.

*Question:* How do you see grief?

*Dr. Hora:* One way to see it is as self-pity, as was mentioned. A full realization that it is the self that hurts can lift us above the self. Another way of approaching grief is through the understanding of human immortality. If we can get a glimpse of that truth, then grief is relieved.

*Comment:* I have been through the greatest personal grief, and I knew absolutely that my loved one was living and was better off, and I had no worry at all on that score. I knew perfectly well that it was personal deprivation that was almost killing me—the desire to be with him again, which was entirely self-gratification, you might say—but the knowledge of that doesn't assuage grief for a long, long time. It has to wear off gradually, but there is no self-delusion in it. The knowledge of eternal life is to me essential to ever really getting over grief, because you know that the other's eternal life is no more eternal than your own, and therefore you can feel that you are both in God's hands. Both lives are in God and are therefore ultimately safe.

*Question:* If grief is only the desire to be with one person—with a particular person—then I should not have felt any grief when I heard that my mother had died at the hands of the Nazis three thousand miles away. I had no possibility of being with her, whether she was still in Vienna, while I was here, or whether she wasn't. It made no real difference. So if grief is only the desire to be with the person, it should have been all the same to me whether she lived or not. But it wasn't.

*Dr. Hora:* Now there are many possibilities and circumstances. Every case of grief would require the elucidation of the personal meaning of the loss of a particular loved one. What is the personal meaning? Some people can get a grief reaction from having a tooth pulled, or from losing money, or whatever. Therefore, we cannot just lay down one single rule to explain everything, but certainly the meaning has a great deal to do with the self.

*Question:* Do you think unmerited suffering is redemptive?

*Comment:* Whether it's redemptive depends upon your reaction to it. Suffering can make one bitter and retaliatory, or it can soften one. You can have all kinds of reactions to it. And whether it is redemptive or not depends on your reaction.

*Dr. Hora:* Yes, just as the distraction we spoke about.

*Question:* Dr. Hora, most philosophical structures have trail-blazers, or saints, or whatever you want to call them. Does yours?

*Dr. Hora:* There is nothing new under the sun, but the understanding of it is forever new in every individual, and that's all that matters. Goethe said, "What you have inherited, you must newly acquire."

*Question:* Isn't this particular orientation new? Isn't existential philosophy very new, too new to have developed saints?

*Dr. Hora:* It may already have martyrs, but I don't know whether there are any saints.

*Question:* Dr. Hora, I was thinking of Suzuki when the previous speaker asked about a saint. I have also been wondering if this concept of complete nothingness—of complete emptiness—is something that can appeal to the Occidental mind. It seems to be the expression of the Buddha and the Tao and so on, and I am wondering if it does have an appeal?

*Dr. Hora:* Good question. Emptiness has little appeal to us because it sounds negative. However, we can say that when the mind is full of love it is completely empty. This is positive and it is also true, and it makes the concept much more acceptable. I think the Buddhist discipline of meditation and prayer is so difficult for us because it tries to accomplish the impossible. Really, we cannot

empty our minds, but love can do it. So what we have to do, if
we want to empty our minds, is to fill them up with love.

*Question:* Isn't there a parable about that—sweep it clean and
all these devils come in?

*Dr. Hora:* Yes, instead of one devil you will get seven devils.
That's right. That's what may be happening in Zen meditation,
at least for some time.

*Question:* I don't want to belabor logotherapy, but I want to
clarify it a bit because Dr. Frankl also had the love theme in addition to the desire to give meaning. His point was that if you
have meaning you can surmount all obstacles. It doesn't seem that
there is much difference. You seem to suggest that this was more
an intellectual process.

*Dr. Hora:* The problem with meaning is this: It is not for us to
give meaning to anything; rather, it is for us to find meaning and
to live by it. Now, it seems that in this particular case a certain
meaning was given, as you would give a pill. Man cannot give
meaning; his task is to discern it and to be transformed by it and
to live by it.

*Question:* How about the word *potential* we hear so much of?
How do you use that word?

*Dr. Hora:* Instead of *potential* you could say *endowment*.

*Question:* Isn't it the integrated self, the potential, what you
think of as your integrated self?

*Dr. Hora:* Potential denotes all the various gifts that each individual is endowed with and that it is his existential task to bring
to fruition. He can accomplish this, or rather this can come about,
if he lives his life the right way. To find the right way is perhaps
the one great meaning and mystery and challenge of every existence.

*Question:* How do you define existential frustration? What differentiates it from other kinds of frustration? Is that pain and
suffering?

*Dr. Hora:* No, it is more a sense of discontent.

*Question:* But does it manifest itself in pain?

*Dr. Hora:* It could, I suppose, but not necessarily. You might be
a cranky person and get into trouble on that basis.

*Question:* Dr. Hora, you mentioned the ineffectuality of the interpersonal approach, yet I believe you have been working in
group psychotherapy. I wonder if you would like to say a word

about the value of group psychotherapy. Most of us think about it as being primarily in the interpersonal sphere.

*Dr. Hora:* Yes, I do work with groups. The traditional group therapies are based on the concept of interaction between sick people who are encouraged to express their sickness in the hope that they might gain insight and learn how to get along with people. In the existential groups the aim is to learn to participate in life situations in a healthy way. The idea is that in order to be healed, man must express healthy concerns. If he is practicing being sick, he will only get sicker. If his concerns are healthy, he will be healed. This corresponds to the biblical passage, *"For whosoever hath, to him shall be given; and whosoever hath not, from him shall be taken even that which he seemeth to have"* (Lk. 8:18). So existential group therapy is a proving ground for wholesome participation in Existence.

*Question:* But isn't there also personal interaction?

*Dr. Hora:* Certainly. Looking at a group from the outside, some people would see personal interaction, but this is not exactly true. The existential group is conceived as participation, for it is assumed that man is not in this world just to have interpersonal relationships; he is in this world to participate in Existence as a beneficial presence. This concept introduces a fundamentally different dimension. If we focus our attention on getting along with people, then we miss the point of Being.

*Comment:* "We are members one of another."

*Dr. Hora:* Yes, that's right. Together we participate in Him, and we live and move and have our being there.

*Question:* It's a form of worship, then, really. You could call it a form of worship.

*Dr. Hora:* That's what life is.

*Essay Five*

# Responsibility

To most people the word *responsibility* carries an unpleasant connotation. It tends to conjure up feelings of burdensomeness, insufficiency, blame, stress and strain, anxiety and worry. Phenomenologically, "responsibility" seems to belong among the unpleasant aspects of life. The main reason for this is the fact that civilized man is conditioned to view responsibility from a purely social, that is, interpersonal, voluntaristic perspective. Thus, parents as representatives of society tend to hold their young children responsible for sphincter control. One of the frequent nightmares of children is connected with the idea of being held responsible for bedwetting. Later on, the child might feel burdened with the responsibility of school performance, and so on. Society may at times demand responses that are not compatible with an individual's physiological and psychological potentialities and capabilities. On the other hand, it may give him undeserved credit for achievements, thus fostering a distorted sense of values concerning personal competence and importance.

The social perspective on responsibility provides man with a false image of human autonomy. In this connection, it is of some interest to note the difference between the Western puppet theaters and the Eastern, notably the Japanese. In the West, the puppets are mostly suspended from above and "animated" by invisible puppeteers who pull strings from behind the scenes and vocalize in such a manner as to create an illusion of maximum independence and self existence of the puppets. The idea is to make the puppets "lifelike." In contrast, the Japanese puppeteer remains in full view of the audience at all times in such a manner as to create the animating background to the puppets, which seem to respond to his will as the foreground. Thus the puppets never seem to lose their connection with their animating source and do not pretend self-existence. They are manifold manifestations and

45

expressions of that power which animates them and which represents the basis of their being.

Both the Western and Eastern puppet theaters may, in a sense, be expressions of their respective views of reality. The Western puppet shows may help the audience forget the puppeteer; the Japanese seem to be concerned with not letting the audience forget his omnipresence. Here the puppeteer and his puppets could be viewed as symbolic of man's inseparability and contingency on his Creator, that is, Existential Ground.

The social perspective places responsibility into the interpersonal dimension and thus relegates it to the discursive sphere of mental activity. Responsibility on a social level is a matter of calculative thought and valuation of the propitious, useful, advantageous, acceptable. Social responsibility appears to revolve around the assertion of human will in the direction of compliance with or defiance of the will of society, which is, after all, composed of other humans. It is, then, a matter of giving in or not giving in, agreeing or disagreeing, cooperating or rebelling. Thus responsibility, when viewed from a social perspective, is characterized by a certain dialectic tension between self and other. It is, then, this tension that lends the word *responsibility* its perennially unpleasant flavor.

If we consider the issue from an existential (ontic) perspective, then responsibility emerges as a mode of being-in-the-world that is primarily concerned with the task of responding to the demands of Existence. At this point two questions arise: What does it mean to respond to the demands of Existence? And how does Existence make its demands known to man?

Existence is that power by virtue of which man exists. Living man bears witness to the existence of Existence. In fact, this is what man seems to be for. In biblical terms, man is the image and likeness of God. Without man God would remain unknown, just as without steel shavings the magnetic field could not be demonstrated. Thus from an ontological standpoint man is responsible to respond to Existence in such a way as to fully demonstrate its nature and reality. Man is a phenomenon of Existence because he sheds light on it, that is, he manifests it.

Existence demands that man be mindful of those conditions under which he can most completely respond to life and realize the potentialities with which he is endowed. The more completely he responds to the demands of Existence in this manner, the more harmonious, wholesome, healthy and peaceable his life becomes. From an ontic perspective, then, responsibility is not a burden but a privilege, it is a life-enhancing, liberating realization. Responsibility (response-ability) here is a God-bestowed ability to respond.

Thus on a social level, responsibility is a rather burdensome task that tends to hamper man's freedom, while on an ontic level it is man's capacity and opportunity to respond to life in order to enjoy its harmonious unfoldment. How can these two contradictory aspects of responsibility be reconciled? The social perspective on responsibility, while relevant to social adaptation, is not directly relevant to and is often in conflict with existential fulfillment. In other words, one may be a socially responsible individual, yet fail to be a wholesome human being. On the other hand, an existentially responsible individual will tend to manifest mental and physical wholesomeness and find little difficulty in rendering "to Caesar the things that are Caesar's" (Mk. 12:17). How is this possible? In attempting to clarify this point, we return to the question concerning the reconciliation of the two contradictory aspects of responsibility.

The difference in the nature of responsibility arises as a consequence of viewing it from two different perspectives, namely, the social and the existential. Man's cognition is greatly determined by his particular perspective on reality. In other words, as man looks at the world, so does it appear to him, for he is inclined to interpret rather than to understand. Consequently, he tends to experience life, not as it really is, but as he thinks it might be or should be. This in turn tends to reinforce his original impressions, in the manner of a feedback mechanism.

The social perspective provides man with a different impression of reality and responsibility than does the existential perspective. Since the existential perspective is broader, it includes the social aspect as well. However, the social perspective, being more narrowly circumscribed, excludes the existential one. Within the social perspective responsibility is a premeditated form of behavior, subject to human calculation. The social perspective is within the domain of the discursive mode of thought.

The existential perspective on life reveals love and reverence to be modes of cognition. Responsibility is man's loving response to Existence (to the will of God). The mode of thought is not calculative-discursive but creative-inspired. Therefore, in the existential perspective man understands rather than interprets. Man is not a self-energizing system but a conscious instrument of a cosmic intelligence. Since he is in cognitive harmony with the truth of what is, he is not separated but in at-one-ment with the flow of life. He is therefore whole (holy), healthy.

## RESPONSIBILITY AND THE SELF

Within the social context of responsibility the sense of the ego is reinforced, for it is the self that confirms and asserts itself by assuming responsibility as well as by neglecting, avoiding or flaunting it. The upright citizen and the beatnik, the conformist and the rebel essentially derive the same sort of gratification from their behavior, namely, the confirmation of their selves. Within the social perspective actions are essentially self-confirmatory, notwithstanding their positive or negative consequences to society. For on a social level one is unselfish for selfish reasons. That which transpires between the self and the other always revolves around the self, for the other is but an other self.

Thus the social perspective on responsibility is a profuse source of disturbances. If man succeeds in living up to his social responsibilities, he tends to feel self-righteously gratified and proud of himself. He is inclined to take credit and feel important. However, this satisfaction is easily turned into despair when he fails or becomes unable to live up to expectations. Within the social context of responsibility man is on a roller coaster of a false sense of importance and an irrational sense of guilt. All this is inevitably accompanied by anxieties, tensions, psychic, somatic, and interpersonal disturbances.

Man living with a false sense of responsibility is like a squeaking rubber doll. When squeezed, the rubber doll becomes deformed and manifests increased inner tension; eventually it will be destroyed. When, however, man discovers the ontic perspective on responsibility, he may experience a release comparable to decompression. His total being will tend to return to a wholesome state. Called "restitutio ad integrum," this is the phenomenon of healing, of becoming that which one truly is and always was.

Within the existential context of responsibility, human actions involve an openness to a higher transcending power. Responsibility becomes a response to that which is not just an other but the very matrix of all that really is. Consequently, existentially responsible man is neither self-assertive, nor self-effacing, nor self-confirmatory. He is responsively life-affirming, truth-revealing and love-manifesting. Existentially responsible man is neither selfish nor unselfish. He is selfless. Above all, he is fearless and loving. Or better yet, he is truly loving, therefore fearless.

Within a social context the existentially responsible man lives, moves and acts as a useful, helpful, beneficent, constructive member of society. He does this, not to confirm his own self or another, but to respond to those fundamental demands of Existence that require him to manifest love, creative intelligence and understanding, and to bear witness to truth under all circumstances. His is a transcending, loving mode of being-in-the-world. To him the good life is not so much a reward as a consequence of responsible living. He reveals Existence as being beyond the duality of reward and punishment.

## RESPONSIBILITY AND SOMA

Human anatomy, biology and physiology are manifestations of Existence within the somatic "field" of phenomena. Within the human organism we can distinguish voluntary and involuntary functions. For instance, the skeletal musculature is an eminently voluntary system, while the actions of the heart, the glands and the digestive system are involuntary. On the surface of things it appears that the human organism by its very nature indicates two modalities, that is, prototypes, of human behavior—namely, that of activity and passivity, self-sufficiency and helplessness, domination and submission, masculinity and femininity.

Within the social perspective on responsibility man has a choice either to assert his will in a responsible fashion or to surrender it. He can be "manly" or "womanly," run his life, or be dependent and passive. There is a pervasive tendency toward a dualistic presupposition about the nature of Existence in general and human function in particular. What is often overlooked is that in reality, Existence is neither fully voluntary nor involuntary, that it is rather a process that requires man to be mindful and reverently responsive (responsible).

One of the most meaningful examples of this is childbirth. Clearly, it is an event in which a woman is required to respond lovingly, reverently, and wholeheartedly to that which is from moment to moment. She can neither assert her will nor remain passive or resistant without hampering the process and suffering painful consequences. Thus, the process of childbirth is a phenomenon of Existence that reveals a significant principle of life. This principle transcends the categories of voluntary and involuntary functions. In fact, we are here introduced to an ontologically determined and organismically manifested value system, the understanding of which becomes the foundation of that religious, philosophical and existential attitude that enables man to attain an optimal realization of his potentialities.

Reverent, loving responsiveness makes it possible for man to minimize conflict and suffering in most aspects of living. It is that form of responsibility which makes the burden of existence light. Existential responsibility is reverence for life in its organismic as well as psychological, social, and spiritual dimensions. Every discordant human experience, whether somatic, individual, interpersonal or social, is characterized by the absence of this fundamental existential attitude to a greater or lesser degree.

Sexuality is one of the more prominent and often more problematic spheres of human experience in which the absence of this transcending mode of being-in-the-world tends to give rise to major psychological, physiological and biological disturbances. When the sexual act is approached from a social-interpersonal perspective, it inevitably becomes an arena for mutual manipulation and exploitation between two individuals, each being concerned with gratifying his own needs to be selfish or generous. Such transactions inevitably leave a sense of discontent in their wake. This tends to set up emotional blocks and inhibitions according to a feedback principle. Within the social perspective sexuality is subjected to the futile and disturbing efforts of voluntary and involuntary controls. This basic misunderstanding of the true nature of life in its sexual manifestation is then the source of a variety of deviations, misuses, abuses, and their psycho-sexual consequences.

The existential perspective reveals sexuality in its spiritual context. In this context, sex transcends the interpersonal subject/object dichotomy and the voluntary/involuntary dualism. It becomes instead a life process in which two individuals participate in an anatomical, biological, physiological, psychological and spiritual complementarity by jointly responding to that which is from moment to moment, which in this case would be the manifestation of Existence in its sexual aspect. Existential responsibility is that mode of responding which invariably transforms the profane by revealing the omnipresence of the sacred.

# Dialogue IV

*Question:* I was thinking, as you were speaking, of statements that have appeared in popular literature about normal people—and find them extremely dull. Is this due to the social modality? If such writers viewed people from the existential standpoint, they would find these people appear differently.

*Dr. Hora:* Well, what is dullness?

*Question:* Well, they weren't constructive in their social activities. They were perfectly well satisfied just to run their homes, to keep up with their neighbors, and weren't too much concerned with anything—they weren't creative people.

*Dr. Hora:* Are there uncreative people? They seem to be, but everyone is creative if he is free. Dullness and uncreativity are signs of mental enslavement of some kind, of lack of freedom. Man needs to be liberated from his mental thralldom for his creative potential to emerge. What is called normal, of course, is a very questionable criterion.

*Dr. Hora restates:* The question is: Can one bring up a child in such a way as to spare him the necessity of laboriously finding his way to harmony with existence?

*Dr. Hora:* The general consensus here seems to be that this is impossible. We must all be born again.

*Question:* How realistic is it to assume that any considerable number of people will or can be born again?

*Dr. Hora:* Statistics have no relevancy here.

*Question:* Would you comment from your own observation as to whether this is actually taking place to any great extent, or is this simply the end goal that everybody should keep in view ultimately?

*Dr. Hora:* I have no way of knowing how much of it is taking place. As far as the goal is concerned, everyone has to decide for himself what his goal in life should be, whether he wants existential fulfillment or perhaps political power or financial success or something else.

*Question:* Suppose one does consciously and earnestly seek this condition of freedom and the realization of love that you spoke of, how realistic is it to imagine that he can attain that condition? Practically, how available is it to most of us?

*Dr. Hora:* You can't measure it. But you see, what seems to be so difficult may not be so difficult. What seems to be so far away is really closer than the air we breathe. We can be changed in the twinkling of an eye.

*Comment from the audience:* I don't think so. (laughter)

*Dr. Hora:* Now, we are very often misled by the appearance of things. We have spoken about certain inclinations to be subjective or objective or analytical. We discussed the tendency to assume that there are two ways to live—actively or passively, masculinely or femininely. This brings to mind an interesting saying attributed to Jesus in the Apocrypha. When asked about the Kingdom of God, he is supposed to have said, "When the two will be one and the inside outside and the male with the female, neither male nor female." Today we were talking about the fact that while life appears to be either voluntary or involuntary, masculine or feminine, active or passive, it isn't really so and it's very hard for us to see that it isn't so. Why is it hard for us to see this? Because we have mental blinders on. Because our assumptions about reality interfere with seeing the truth. We have to learn to see right and to discover that reality is nondual, as the Oriental philosophers say. It is nondual, which means it is neither voluntary nor involuntary. And we have beautiful examples of it, as I mentioned to you, for instance, in childbirth. There are other examples too. In the process of childbirth, complications arise usually from the woman's having an erroneous notion as to how to respond to this situation. Some may be too active and some too passive. If a woman too actively asserts her will, she can damage herself or the child by pressing too hard and being too anxious and becoming cramped. If a woman is too passive, she may damage herself or the child because she delays the process by not participating properly. The most favorable condition for a healthy delivery is when the woman's state of consciousness is loving, reverent, joyous, wholeheartedly responsive. She is fully there. It is interesting that the First Commandment is worded very similarly: *"Thou shalt love the Lord thy God with all thy heart, and with all thy soul, and with all thy strength, and with all thy mind"* (Lk. 10:27). As long as we are glorifying self-assertiveness, we are based on the notion of voluntarism. The result is that one minute we are self-assertive, the next minute we are self-restraining and self-effacing, or both at the same time, which is even more complicated.

*Question.* What about the observations so often made of the saints of old and people who have been great thinkers and achievers, and deeply spiritual: that in their early lives they were apt to have been pretty wild and to have sown their wild oats and then been converted?

*Dr. Hora:* You mean, the wilder they are, the sooner the "twinkle" comes? (laughter) This "twinkling" usually comes when we run into a so-called existential crisis, when things don't work out anymore. We are up against a wall and that's very often the time when we reconsider everything and are forced to view life from a different perspective.

*Question:* How can a selfless existentialist become a competitive contractor?

*Dr. Hora:* I don't think an existentialist would be a competitive contractor. He might try to be a good one.

*Comment:* He would go bankrupt.

*Dr. Hora:* That is possible. (laughter)

*Comment:* Lawyers don't have a very good reputation as a rule, but I know a Quaker lawyer who, when his problems became a little difficult, would put his secretary out of the room and lie on the floor until his consciousness was that which we are speaking of and he would know his problems were solved. It is perfectly practical for people to lead busy lives in a profession and still have a moment now and again to realize their unity with God and lead a spiritual life. The two things don't have to be separated at all.

*Dr. Hora:* What many people don't realize is the practical value of prayer. It is much better than competition—and more effective, too. But to know how to pray is another issue.

*Question:* How would you explain the commandment *"Thou shalt love thy neighbor as thyself"* (Lk. 10:27), meaning you should love yourself, which is a stumbling block if you think you should be selfless?

*Dr. Hora:* No, it is only a stumbling block as long as you think you should be a self.

*Question:* How can you love it if it isn't there?

*Dr. Hora:* To love is to know aright. To love your neighbor as your self is only possible if you know him and your self aright. In order to be loving we have to know the truth about the self. And the truth about the self is that it is a lie. When we know that, then it is easy to love our neighbor because we don't love his personality or character structure, we love his being.

*Comment:* I have learned to think of it as the I and I AM, the I representing all that is negative. Whenever we have any negative feelings or emotions of any kind whatsoever, that is the I—as against the I AM as it was revealed to Moses—I am that I AM. It's this I AM in us that is always constructive.

*Dr. Hora:* That's very good.

*Question:* How is this applied to an intimate relationship such as that between husband and wife. In an intimate relationship, if we feel that we have attained a measure of this realization and the other person hasn't, we tend to rebel against being used as a thing. Does this rebellion stem from the feeling of being threatened, and does this indicate that we have not attained a sufficient degree of it to handle it comfortably?

*Dr. Hora:* One of the great stumbling blocks in our culture is the tremendous emphasis on the word *relationship*. This word gives a certain slant to our outlook on life. It immediately puts self and others into the picture and it implies some sort of transaction. To illustrate, I like to compare it with dancing—ballroom dancing. If you are a poor dancer, then you have a relationship with your partner. You keep stepping on each other's toes. Right? But if you are really good dancers then you don't have a relationship anymore, you are just participating in harmonious movement to the music. And so it is in life. We may be poor dancers and deaf to boot. If we don't know how to live, we have relationships with people. We also try to have a relationship with God but God doesn't lend himself to a relationship. He requires at-one-ment. When we understand Existence, we become participants and we transcend the need for relationships. And the same goes for marriage. As long as marriage is a relationship, the partners step on each other's toes. The ideal conception of marriage is that it is a joint participation of two individuals who can complement each other and together form a creative unit. That makes it simple and harmonious.

*Question:* What happens when one partner is a good dancer and the other partner is a lousy dancer?

*Dr. Hora:* Then you have a relationship.

*Question:* But what do you do with it?

*Dr. Hora:* Then you try to be so beneficial as to eventually form it into a joint participation.

*Question:* When you say the two individuals complement each other, do you mean they are different from one another in their ideas?

*Dr. Hora:* A key and a lock are different but they complement each other beautifully.

*Question:* But isn't it much easier when opinions and main ideals are the same rather than different?

*Dr. Hora:* Complementarity does not imply different existential goals. If the two are not complementary but similar, for a while they may enjoy each other's company, but after a while they become rivals.

# Wholeness

The word *wholeness* is synonymous with *completeness*. It denotes a condition where nothing is missing. It refers to an object, a situation, or a state of being that is devoid of any defect. The word *wholeness* implies perfection. Within the phenomenal world wholeness in the sense of perfection does not exist. And even if it existed, we would be unable to perceive it since our perceptive equipment is in itself imperfect. Only perfection could see perfection. Yet, in the Bible we read, *"Be ye therefore perfect even as your Father which is in heaven is perfect"* (Matt. 5:48). The Bible also speaks of *"perfect love"* that *"casteth out fear"* (1 Jn. 4:18). Further, we are told that holiness is synonymous with wholeness, and wholeness in man denotes healthiness. All this is etymologically related to the word *healing*. *"Behold, thou art made whole"* (Jn. 5:14), said Jesus to the man who was sick of the palsy.

Healing then is a mysterious process through which man becomes whole, healthy. But what has all this to do with holiness? We are accustomed to thinking of holiness in religious terms. Holiness has become closely associated in our thinking with piousness. Piousness, however, on closer inspection may often turn out to be a form of superstitious ritualism, or obsessive-compulsive neurosis, or just plain hypocrisy. It seems therefore desirable to salvage the term *holiness* from its primarily religious connotation and redefine it in its existential context. From an existential standpoint, holiness is a mode of being-in-the-world that is centered around the concern with wholeness as existential fulfillment. Existential fulfillment does not mean "living it up to the hilt" until we have had our fill of existence, but rather being concerned with fulfilling our mission in life by bringing to fruition our inherent potentialities.

All manifestations of life seem to be endowed with the task of running their course to the end. What is called the instinct of self-preservation may well be a built-in tendency toward existential holiness, which is concerned with completing each existence, thus making it whole. While in the animal kingdom existence seems to be prevalently biological and very much determined, in man it is a more complex process because he is endowed with a higher form of consciousness. Consciousness is then the central issue in human fulfillment. While all living creatures seem to be unconsciously or instinctively holy, man is required to seek wholeness consciously. If he fails in his task, he experiences existential anxiety and frustration. Furthermore, he may evolve a variety of misdirected modes of being-in-the-world, the symptoms of which are known as diseases of mind and body.

The quest for wholeness tends to take place on three different levels: (1) the subjective; (2) the objective; and (3) the existential. On the subjective level, man seeks to attain wholeness through so-called emotional health. An individual living on this level pays a great deal of attention to how he feels. He tries to keep his feelings in proper balance by controlling their intensity, quality, and expression. He also endeavors to use his feelings as a cognitive apparatus by trying to understand reality through his emotions. He tries to feel what others feel and thus, by empathizing, he either sympathizes or antipathizes. The attention of the subjectivist is focused on the self. He is subject to the vicissitudes of self-consciousness with its possible ramifications, from mild forms of egotism to hysterical tendencies, all the way to severe hypochondriasis. Subjectivism is a misdirected mode of being-in-the-world.

The second level on which man seeks wholeness is the objective. The objectivist seeks to live his life by mastery of the outer world. While the subjectivist is endeavoring to control his inner world of personal experience, the objectivist is striving to fulfill his life by mastery of the outer world. His is a materialistic view of reality. His world is a conglomeration of objects, data and facts. He tends to treat people as things to be handled and controlled; as a consequence, he often creates the impression of being tyrannical. Since he is concerned with mastery and power, his attention is inescapably centered around his own self. Thus, the objectivist is inevitably self-centered, even if his motives are altruistic. He tends to be intellectual and analytical. He can be unselfish only in selfish ways.

The intellectual seeks to fulfill his existence through analytical reasoning in terms of causality and motivation. He attempts to fulfill himself by trying to find out what makes people tick and why things are the way they are. The world of the intellectual revolves around cause-and-effect thinking, and the pride of learning. Everything and everyone represents a challenge, an object to be figured out, diagnosed and interpreted as an effect resulting from a hypothetical cause. Since, to be intellectual, all things and beings are just analytical material, he centers his attention around his own thought potential. Consequently, as an intellectual the objectivist is inevitably self-centered. He often creates an impression of being cruel because he tends to take people apart and to be an expert in fault-finding.

Thus we see that the subjectivist is self-centered in his emotions, the objectivist in his quest for mastery and in his reasoning power. The consciousness in these modes of being-in-the-world is centered around the self.

Now, what's wrong with being self-centered? Self-centered consciousness cannot attain to wholeness because it is not conscious of the whole of reality. Self-centered man is the victim of a cognitive deficiency. His focus is partial and fragmented. To illustrate, let us take a flower as an example. To the subjectivist a flower may be not much more than a source of olfactory or visual gratification. To the objectivist it may be a decorative or an otherwise useful object or it may be a botanical specimen of scientific interest. But to a whole man it may be a "smile of God," a symbol of aesthetic value, an expression of the presence of beauty and harmony in the world.

This brings to mind the famous flower sermon once preached by Gautama, the Buddha, before a large gathering. He held up a flower, but said nothing. In the entire gathering only one man understood the sermon, and Buddha discerned it by his smile. This man, Ananda, later became Buddha's successor. It is interesting to note that the communication between Buddha and Ananda on that occasion was nonverbal and the sign was a smile. This means that it was not an intellectual, conceptual message, but an existential communication. We could conjecture that the quality of Ananda's presence in the situation conveyed to the Buddha the following: "A flower is a smile of God, and the smile of the enlightened man is a witness to it, because man is an image and likeness of God."

Furthermore, we can say that the subjectivist is concerned with pleasure, the objectivist with power and with intellectual learning, the holy man with existential worshiping, which means witnessing.

Wholeness entails a cognitive integration that is not only physical, emotional, intellectual, social, and environmental, but ontic-existential as well. That means that in order for a man to be healthy, his cognitive faculty must make it possible for him to be in harmony with the Fundamental Order of Being. To this end he must endeavor to broaden his consciousness to the point of attaining the ontic-existential perspective, which we designated as the third level on which man seeks wholeness. The ontic perspective transcends all other levels and integrates them into a wholesome state of consciousness.

While the first two levels of concern tend to be mutually exclusive, partial and fragmented, the ontic-existential concern is all-inclusive and holistic, wholesome. Thus, we can define wholeness as a mode of being-in-the-world that is characterized by a consciousness centered not around the self but around Existence.

What is Existence? Existence is that power by virtue of which man exists and which he manifests. Man bears witness to the existence of Existence. The endeavor to view all aspects of life, not from the subjective or objective and intellectual standpoints, but from the ontic perspective, brings human consciousness into harmony with Existence. Such consciousness constitutes the basis for existential wholeness, holiness, healthiness, true maturity.

This wholeness then becomes manifest as a presence. This presence is characteristically fearless, loving, peaceful, intelligent, creative and beneficial. It is devoid of arrogance, pride, guilt and anxiety. We could say that true wholeness is a spiritual attribute of man that underlies and determines all other aspects of his being, and that is attained through an epistemological development of his consciousness.

Epistemology is the study of the nature of knowledge. It concerns itself with the exploration of the processes whereby man arrives at knowledge. Furthermore, epistemology studies the relevance of knowing to being. Adam and Eve partook of the tree of knowledge. Socrates believed that the source of this wisdom and the essence of his being was the knowing of his not knowing. The Delphic oracle proclaims, "Know thyself!" The Zen Buddhist and the Taoist sages are quoted as having said, "He who knows doesn't know, and he who doesn't know knows." A Zen disciple is reported to have exclaimed in the moment of his enlightenment, "The bottom of the pail has broken through," thus indicating that in his own consciousness, his attitude toward his mental content had undergone a sudden and radical change. And finally, Jesus said, *"Ye shall know the truth and the truth shall make you free"* (Jn. 8:32).

We see then that wholeness is an epistemological issue since it depends on a particular mode of knowing. We are also impressed by the discovery that there are modes of knowing that interfere with wholeness, as was pointed out in connection with subjectivity and objectivity. These modes of knowing apparently cannot comprehend the truth. Jesus emphasized the importance of knowing the truth. In other words, he implied that the right kind of knowing is that which is capable of discerning the truth. Such knowledge liberates. From what? From errors of interpretation and their consequences. And how can we know that this is so? We know it by the fruits. The fruits of right knowing are freedom, wholeness, harmony, understanding.

To illustrate, let us take the example of a parent and his child. Suppose the parent has a subjectivistic attitude toward his child. Such a parent reveals a concern with how his child "makes him feel." In other words, he focuses his attention on how his own feelings and emotions are stimulated, gratified or frustrated by his child's behavior. In the eyes of the child, this could take on a variety of meanings. He might see the parent as egocentric, seductive, even incestuous.

Should the parent's attitude be an objectivistic one, he might reduce his child to a thing, objectifying him in his concern with mastery and control. This may produce in the child a loss of his sense of human worth.

Should the parent be intellectually inclined as well, he would be likely to generate a great deal of anxiety, indecision and confusion by interpreting causes and motives for his child's behavior. Such an intellectual-psychologizing perspective may engender a variety of tendencies, from exaggerated intellectual self-preoccupation to self-conscious inhibition, from loss of spontaneity conceivably all the way to catatonic rigidity or paranoid schizophrenia.

Subjectivist parents tend to bring up selfish, hypochondriacal, sexually over-stimulated and hedonistic children. Objectivist parents often appear tyrannical and their children tend to become recalcitrant and rebellious, while analytical and psychologizing parents may well be a source of schizophrenic reactions in the family.

It is the loving parent who understands. Why is this so? Because love is that state of consciousness that focuses attention on truth and beneficence. Love, then, is a mode of cognition, a way of knowing. True love is that mode of knowing which makes it possible for man to discern the truth of a situation and to respond to it in a wholesome manner.

Other conditions that signal lack of wholeness in man are competition, rivalry, and intermittent ascendancy of the senses, the emotions or the intellect. Some people are prevalently sensuous, or emotional, or intellectual; others are more or less permanently fixated in one of these three faculties; still others keep shifting from one to another; then there are those who expend a great deal of effort in maintaining a proper balance among the three. Such balance is like an uneasy peace based on a treaty constantly in danger of being violated. It is a form of coexistence characterized by competitive cooperation, or cooperative rivalry, among three powers. At best, it is an uneasy truce, always in danger of disbalance and eruption of conflict.

In this connection, it is interesting to contemplate the symbolism of the three Kings (heads of states) coming to the manger in Bethlehem. Led by a star pointing the way, the rulers of the kingdom of the senses, the kingdom of the emotions and the kingdom of the intellect come to the Harmonizing Principle of Existence and find the peace of the Kingdom of God. In the context of wholeness, this would indicate the significance of spiritual love, which must be man's orientation and overriding concern if he is to become an integrated, harmonious being, capable of knowing and expressing genuine peace rather than just a precarious balance called "ego control."

Wholeness expresses itself as harmonious action and response. Harmonious response is spontaneity; spontaneity is an aspect of grace that is intimately related to understanding and responding. The subjectivist and the objectivist intellectual know neither grace nor spontaneity for they do not respond, but rather react. Theirs is not a responsive, responsible life; theirs is a reactive existence.

The following story illustrates this point. A young mother left her baby in her carriage outside a store and went inside to shop.

When she returned, she noticed that two elderly men had brought the baby indoors and were playing with her. The mother heard one of the men remark that it was snowing outside, and since the baby was crying, they had brought her indoors. At this, the mother became angry, berated the two men and left in a huff, to be upset the rest of the day. In other words, she was unable to respond intelligently and with grace to the situation; rather, she reacted to an implied or fancied criticism of how she fulfilled her role as a mother. Her perspective was a subjective one. She did not discern the fact that gratitude was in order for the loving solicitude expressed for her infant. She did not respond to love and truth, but rather reacted to self and others. A thorough analysis of this experience helped her to glimpse the fact that in the realm of grace there is neither self nor other, but only that which really is.

Wholeness makes it possible for man to respond harmoniously because the loving mode of cognition enables him to know understandingly. Thus, the epistemological approach to wholeness embraces the totality of human existence. It leads to ontic integration. Ontic integration denotes a mode of being where man is not merely an integrated personality, or a socially well-adjusted person, or an emotionally balanced individual, or a sexually mature male or female, but a harmonious being whose presence in the world is a beneficial one.

If we consider the therapeutic and redemptive implications of all that was said, we are amazed to find a great deal of overlapping between psychotherapy, religion, and Oriental philosophy, with epistemology providing the missing link. In view of all this, prayer and meditation can be understood as the means through which the attainment of wholeness is sought.

Prayer and meditation thus become disciplines by which man endeavors to rise above subjectivistic and objectivistic-intellectual modes of thought. By thus expanding and purifying his consciousness, he learns to see life from an ontic-existential perspective and to know that truth which liberates him by making him whole.

# Prayer

We are accustomed to thinking of prayer as a devotional act or an endeavor to communicate with a power believed to be of vital personal significance. From the standpoint of mental health, we can, broadly speaking, distinguish the following erroneous modes of prayer:

1. Ritualistic prayer is motivated either by superstitious, fearful, and magical thinking of a primitive mind or underdeveloped consciousness, or by social hypocrisy and conformism. In the first instance, it is designed to gain favor with primitive and usually wrathful gods; in the second instance, it is a quest for status in a community of like-minded people.
2. Intellectual prayer is a species of mental vanity indulging itself in pretty phraseology and verbiage.
3. Emotional prayer is mostly self-indulgent wallowing in emotion under the pretext of piety.
4. Sensuous prayer is very close to emotional prayer, except that here sensory stimuli, as, for instance, flagellation or other forms of mortification of the flesh, are in the foreground of interest.

The term *ceaseless prayer,* however, connotes abiding; it implies something continuous, a way of life, a mode of being. We could define ceaseless prayer as a persistent endeavor to actualize the loving mode of being-in-the-world. It is a continuous process of mental purification based on a desire to correct false assumptions and concepts, erroneous concerns, and misdirected orientations. Therefore, it is a cognitive form of prayer, constituting what we call existential worship.

Meditation can be considered a cognitive form of prayer preparatory to existential worship, for meditation is a process of mental purification (mind-fasting) that consists of turning away from a set mental attitude in order to reach a realization of the presence of God as harmony, peace, and love-intelligence.

Existential worship is prayer in action. This action, however, is to be differentiated from activity; it is also to be differentiated from passivity. Existential worship is neither active nor passive. It is neither voluntary nor involuntary. It is reverential, responsive, cognitive. It is not calculated, but is motivated by a "hunger and thirst" for understanding the truth of Existence, the truth of God, his universe, and man's place in it. It is reverential because reverence is a sincerely receptive attitude. It is responsive because it does not originate in man. It is cognitive because it takes place in man's consciousness. The condition of a man's consciousness reveals itself by the quality of his presence in the world. A consciousness that is in harmony with Existence, that is reverential and responsive to the will of God, or the Fundamental Order of Being, reveals itself as a loving, intelligent, and beneficial presence.

Such a presence lives and moves and has its being in a relatively friendly world where seeming obstacles, problems, and difficulties tend to dissolve with relative ease, and where peace and wisdom prevail, for *"as he thinketh in his heart, so is he"* (Prov. 23:7). What a man thinks in his heart is his secret desire, and it tends to determine his way of experiencing life. Someone said: "We think in secret and it comes to pass—the world is but our looking glass."

Jesus' teaching about prayer is of great relevance here. In Matthew 6:6 we read: *"When thou prayest, enter into thy closet, and when thou has shut the door, pray to the Father which is in secret; and thy Father which seeth in secret shall reward thee openly."*

In considering these two quotations, we are immediately impressed by their emphasis on secrecy. The poet speaks of thinking in secret, and the Bible speaks of praying in secret. Furthermore, we read that God is in secret and sees in secret. The question then arises, What is the significance of this emphasis on secrecy? We can discover the meaning of it if we consider the fact that it is the nature of a secret to be treasured. Secrets must be treasured whether or not they are liked or hated, desired or feared. The chief characteristic of all secrets is that they are treasured. In epistemological terms we can say that our secrets constitute our abiding concerns; that is, whatever attracts or captures our abiding concern becomes our god. In view of all this, we can say that man is an eminently prayerful creature. However, he tends to have a large choice of gods that he can worship. The question of prayer then is not whether or not to pray, but what to pray to and how.

A young man remarked: "Whenever I try to pray, I always have the feeling that my prayers are falling on deaf ears. God never seems to hear me. Prayer seems utterly useless." In answer to this, it was pointed out to him that he thought of God as someone with ears. This surprised him for he knew that anthropomorphizing God is a mistake, but he couldn't see an alternative. It was then pointed out to him that prayer is not an attempt to catch God's ear in order to tell him what he should do for us, but rather an endeavor to bring our consciousness into a condition where we can hear what God has to say to us. Prayer is a method, not of influencing God, but of being influenced by him.

One thing is now clear, namely, that all gods are secret gods and that under ordinary circumstances all worship takes place in the secrecy of our "closet," that is, our consciousness. However, the Bible says that "God, which is in secret and seeth in secret" rewards us openly. The secret gods that man treasures in the secrecy of his fantasies, daydreams, yearnings, and fears become manifest in the quality of his presence in the world and thus, in turn, shape his experience and, to a large extent, his destiny. I think it was Freud who said that character is destiny.

At this point, two questions come to mind. First, if all prayer and worship is in secret, what value is there in open, conscious, and public worship? The answer is that open, conscious, and public worship seems of little value unless it is a joint endeavor of like-minded individuals to lend each other support in finding the right God to worship. This support may to a large extent be nonverbal and can be communicated existentially, namely, through the quality of participation.

The second question may be put as follows: Is the effect of prayer limited to characterological consequences, or, as we put it, does it only affect the quality of man's presence? When, through prayer, the right kind of presence is attained, this mode of being becomes a door through which limitless possibilities of good can enter into human experience, both individually and collectively.

A third question may be asked: How does intercessory prayer, that is, prayer for the welfare of others, fit into the cognitive concept of worship? It would seem at first glance that praying for the welfare of others inevitably entails petitioning God, that is, trying to influence him to do something for someone. This, of course, has been practiced since time immemorial in all religions, but its effectiveness is questionable. For any endeavor to influence God presupposes an anthropomorphic deity, and inevitably leads into the ritualistic, or intellectual, or emotional, or sensuous modes of worship. Nevertheless, it is undeniable that intercessory prayer can be effective. How can this be? It is easy to understand that a beneficial presence benefits all those around it, even without any intentional verbal contact. There are those who are a joy to be near. It may even be understandable that some people's presence is a blessing to an entire group or household, even a community. Somehow their beneficial consciousness tends to spread and harmonize the affairs of those in a large area. Something about human consciousness transcends time and space. A consciousness that is in harmony with God, or cosmic intelligence, may conceivably extend its beneficial impact beyond temporo-spatial considerations. Thus, it is conceivable that intercessory prayer in this sense may be effective in large measure and in proportion to man's capacity to bring his consciousness into harmony with divine Love-Intelligence.

It seems that our prayers are always answered. Unfortunately, more often than not we pray in erroneous ways for wrong things and to false gods. Job said: *"For the thing which I greatly feared is come upon me"* (Job 3:25). And Emerson is known to have said, "Beware of what you set your heart on, for you will surely get it."

A talented young man was for years afflicted with abject poverty, despite his strenuous efforts to get ahead in life and provide for his wife and child. One day he discovered that he was secretly devoted to a dream of somehow getting money from an elderly rich lady who might pity him. His secret devotion caused him to assume a pitiful, poverty-stricken appearance, since how else could his dream come true? In other words, the quality of his presence in this world was determined by his prayers. When Freud called neurosis a private religion, he was right; but when he jumped to the conclusion that all religious concerns are neurotic, he was tragically mistaken.

The young man considered himself positively atheistic and antireligious. When confronted with his private religion, he thought that this discovery would at least justify his original antireligious bias. However, before long he had to face the fact that the alternative to his dilemma was not atheism but a more intelligent, wholesome life of devotion.

Interestingly, false gods can be worshiped positively or negatively, but the true God can be worshiped only through love. This means that the true God is one God. This God is nondual Ultimate Reality. The nondual reality of the true God requires man to worship existentially, namely, with his being, or better yet with his "I AM," since God proclaimed himself to Moses as *"I AM that I AM"* (Ex. 3:14). Since the basic attribute of this God is love—and the First Commandment demands an abiding love—the proper existential mode of worship could be described as the love of being loving.

To illustrate, let us consider the story of a married couple who experienced considerable discord in the area of sex. The husband thought sex to be very important; the wife thought it distasteful. The situation grew from bad to worse, and the marriage reached an impasse. It became clear that they were worshiping the same false god, one positively, the other negatively. Having seen this to be true, they were led to shift their concern about love to an existential plane and thus worship the real God. Then *"all things work together for good"* (Rom. 8:28) since they loved God.

A young mother of three sought psychiatric treatment for a number of reasons, among them depression, chain smoking, irritability, and excessive daydreaming. She soon revealed an intense bitterness against her husband, whom she described as unkind and cruel in his attitude toward her. They caused each other a great deal of pain. They worshiped each other, but in a negative way. When things became intolerable, they decided to try "free love" as a solution to their misery; each found himself several lovers, and they proceeded to engage in adulterous activities. On weekends, they would tell each other about their exploits. For a time it seemed that things were improving, except that the woman's chain smoking persisted, her depression recurred, and her daydreams never ceased. Her husband had his own set of symptoms. Soon it became clear that the so-called free love was no remedy but was only another ritual in the false devotion to vengeful, negative worship. Healing required the patient to turn away from worshiping her husband, positively or negatively. Only by worshiping God existentially, that is, only by devoting herself to a different kind of "free love"—the real free love that means *"freely you have received, freely give"* (Matt. 10:8)—could this young woman regain her health, her freedom and her marriage.

Cigarette smoking may be viewed as a form of positive and negative worshiping. A smoker loves to smoke and hates it at the same time. Cigarette smoking indicates a mode of being-in-the-world that is centered around the concern for comfort. The cigarette smoker smokes when he is tense in order to relax, and he smokes when he is relaxing in order to enjoy feeling comfortable. He smokes when he feels bad and he smokes when he feels good. His concern is with his feelings, with his personal comfort. Existential worshiping introduces a shift of emphasis from personal comfort to participating in Existence as a beneficial presence. Here feeling good becomes, so to speak, a by-product of being good rather than an artificial state induced by cigarettes, drugs, alcohol or other means. It is important to know that our concerns determine the quality of our presence in the world, and thus shape our individual destinies. When we think about it, all this seems so simple and so self-evident that we are tempted to say, "Why belabor the obvious?" And yet it is amazing how easily we can be sidetracked from remembering it. A good example is seen in the Oedipus myth.

The story of Oedipus, as it unfolds in the Greek tragedy written by Sophocles, is briefly as follows: When Oedipus was born, his parents, King Laius and Queen Jocasta, were told a frightful prophecy: that the boy would kill his father and marry his mother. The parents became so frightened of this prophecy that they abandoned their son. He was saved and raised by another king as his own son. As the boy grew, he began to doubt his parentage. When he learned about the prophecy, he became frightened and left his foster parent's home. His flight led him to an encounter with an unknown man at a place where three highways met. Here, he inadvertently got into a quarrel with the man and killed him. The man, of course, was King Laius. Oedipus then married Laius's wife, his own mother.

It is well known that Freud interpreted the meaning of this tragedy as proof of man's universal tendency to be incestuously attracted to his mother and to harbor murderous impulses toward his father. He thus arrived at the formulation of the theory of the Oedipus complex.

The theory of the Oedipus complex has become a subject of widespread controversy. Interestingly enough, the more people wondered about its validity and argued about it, the easier it became for all to see it in the lives of most people. In other words, even if one was against it, he was also for it because he was involved with it.

This in itself is a very startling phenomenon, relevant to our discussion. Advertising people have known for a long time that it doesn't matter whether they please their prospective customers or irritate them, the important thing is to capture their attention and to implant an idea into their minds.

The first great challenge to Freud's theory of the Oedipus complex came from Heidegger. The famous contemporary philosopher proposed a revision of the Oedipus myth by interpreting the tragedy as a consequence of man's quest for knowledge. He suggested that Oedipus was driven, not by sexual instinct toward his mother, but by a hunger to know the truth about himself.

Rebecca M. Osborn has made another, beautiful interpretation of the Oedipus story.[4] She endeavored to show that the tragedy of Oedipus was rooted in parental neglect, notably the failure of his mother, Jocasta, to fulfill her responsibility to her child, of showing him that she had faith in him, notwithstanding the prophecy. Mrs. Osborn concluded: "Laius, of course, was also responsible for the abandoning of Oedipus, but the act seems more unnatural on the part of the mother whose purpose is to nurture and protect the children she bears."

In the context of our discussion we can now arrive at a fourth possibility regarding the meaning of this Greek tragedy. Namely, by considering it from an epistemological standpoint, we are immediately impressed by a self-evident factor that was overlooked in the three previous interpretations, that is, prophecy.

What is a prophecy? Prophecies and curses are significant concerns implanted in man's consciousness. As such, they become personal gods, feared and hated, believed in, desired, surrendered to, or opposed. If fought against, they are clung to and thus inadvertently worshiped. What man worships, he lives by and also dies by. We can thus discover that the epistemological meaning of the Oedipus myth is a family tragedy brought about by a prophecy, accepted into consciousness and then fought against worshipfully. In the words of the poet, it was a "secret thought which came to pass." The question may now be asked, What lesson is there for us in considering the Oedipus myth from the standpoints of its substance, its essence, and its various interpretations?

First of all, we had to consider its substance in order to extricate its essence. Having done so, we discovered the danger of accepting prophecies and false concerns into our consciousness. This teaches us the great value of epistemological prayer whereby we can free our minds of unwholesome content by turning toward existentially wholesome concerns. This means "conversion" to the loving mode of being-in-the-world and participation in Existence as a beneficial presence. In other words, existential worship liberates man from his mental bondage; it would have saved Oedipus and his parents from what, in their time, was considered a sealed, inalterable fate.

The range of interpretations of the Oedipus myth is very significant because it illustrates a universal human tendency to search for causes and reasons rather than for meanings, and to narrow our focus rather than open it up wide to behold reality from an ontic-existential spiritual perspective.[5]

# Dialogue V

*Question:* Don't you feel that some of these other prayers you have spoken of are helpful in moving toward the right kind of prayer? For example, I have in mind the sensuous method. Incense and stained glass windows are sensuous, but aren't they of assistance in getting a person into the right mood for being at one with God?

*Dr. Hora:* Yes, they could be, provided we don't stop there. If we look at prayer as an integrative process, that is, from the standpoint of psychiatry rather than of religion, then the proper understanding of the various obstacles that stand in the way of effective prayer can help us to get beyond these. For it is possible to spend years deluding oneself that one is religious or that one is praying, and never really discover the truth about prayer as meaningful consciousness of the reality of God. God can remain a theory, a social convention, a probability, a symbol, and never become an existential reality. Now, this has always been a problem, and it still most certainly is. Our aim is to better understand prayer in all its aspects, and particularly in its relevance to wholesome existence. We are also interested in its social and therapeutic implications. We could say that in order to be able to pray effectively, we have to reach a certain level of wholeness. This in turn implies that the healthier we are, the more health we can partake in. The more wholesome we are, the more wholesome and holy we can become. This reminds us that " . . . *to everyone that hath shall be given, and he shall have abundance: but from him that hath not shall be taken away even that which he hath*" (Matt. 25:29).

The human condition reveals a built-in problem—man's inclination to get stuck on the sensuous, the emotional, or the intellectual level, or to fluctuate among these three, or to try to achieve a certain balance among them. In psychology we speak of being well balanced, emotionally balanced, balancing our feelings against our intellect. Years have been spent, and numerous books have been written, on ways and means of bringing about this kind

73

of balance. This balance is called personality integration, or ego control, or emotional maturity. However, that which is balanced is balancing, and that which is balancing is always precarious.

*Question:*   What philosophy would be considered the opposite of existentialism?

*Dr. Hora:*   Most everything. Every time this comes up, some people tend to get upset. The important thing to know is that ideas need not be accepted, nor do they need to be rejected; they need to be seen. The general tendency is to think dualistically, which means that we tend to think in terms of "Do I agree with this, or do I disagree with it? Do I accept it, or do I reject it?" Here is where epistemology comes in. As long as we think dualistically—in terms of accepting or rejecting, agreeing or disagreeing—our consciousness is incapable of understanding; whatever understanding develops happens in spite of our dualistic thought. Understanding is a peculiar mental process that depends on a certain attitude toward truth, namely, a reverent, receptively responsive attitude that is neither acquisitive nor rejecting but waits for truth to reveal itself. A wonderful thing happens to man when he learns to refrain from the habit of agreeing or disagreeing. I would compare it to the liberation of the mind from a straitjacket. Or we could say that an individual who has learned to go beyond accepting and rejecting, agreeing and disagreeing, is like a chrysalis that has become a butterfly. The thinking of such an individual gains new vitality. He is suddenly mentally free and is not tense about what people say. It does not matter what kinds of ideas people may proffer, whether communistic, or atheistic, or crazy, or challenging. They will not be a problem to him because he will not be confronted with the necessity of deciding whether to agree or disagree, to accept or reject them. His concern is only to see whatever reveals itself. He is grateful for whatever dawns upon his consciousness, and he is not upset about what he does not understand. A Zen disciple described this freedom in the following way: "The bottom of the pail has broken through!"

*Comment:*   That's the fundamental Quaker view in a way—waiting for what comes up within you.

*Dr. Hora:*   Yes. This is an important process of mental liberation and often constitutes the first few weeks in psychotherapy. Patients invariably have to learn to hear what is being said, without trying to acquire it or reject it, or agree with it or disagree with it. Now, this may sound to some like an attitude of "I don't care," but it must not be confused with indifference. It is an attitude of reverence for that which reveals itself, reverence for truth.

*Comment:* It is helpful to me to recognize that many of these theological problems that might be argued about are really inventions of the human mind. Somewhere along the line we have been indoctrinated into thinking they had to be solved, or they were major premises or something of that nature.

*Dr. Hora:* Yes. You see, to the sensuous man God is sensation; to the emotional man God is a feeling; to the intellectual man God is a concept; to the ritualistic man God is a fear. But to the loving man God is real. That means he is neither abstract nor concrete. For the abstract is that which is thinkable, and the concrete is that which is tangible. God is neither thinkable nor tangible. God is life. This is where existentialism comes in. Existence, likewise, is neither thinkable nor tangible; therefore, Existence is synonymous with God. And it depends on what level of cognitive development we exist, what God means to us. This is why it helps to know that it is possible to reach a state of consciousness in which we can apprehend that which is neither abstract nor concrete. We can discern the nonthinkable.

*Comment:* I am impressed by your reference to Moses' experience of the presence of God on the mountain when he asks, "What name shall I say?" And the answer is, "I AM THAT I AM," or "I am who I am or what I am."

*Dr. Hora:* That's the beginning of existentialism.

*Question:* Could you come back for a moment to your reference to different types of prayer and comment again on the subject of intercessory prayer in this context?

*Dr. Hora:* All right, let us consider your question. You ask, "Is it possible for one individual to pray for another?" The answer is as follows: It is being done and I think it is being done with some effectiveness, but the question remains, How can we understand it within the point of view that has been presented here? Right?

*Comment:* It wouldn't be a prayer having anything specific in mind, since that would be intellectual. We wouldn't know what the other person really needed, anyway.

*Dr. Hora:* That's right.

*Comment:* And yet that doesn't negate the fact that one can pray for another.

*Dr. Hora:*   I believe that it is possible. You see, here we are confronted with the necessity of getting beyond the individual. We have to consider the following question: Where are the boundaries of consciousness? Is consciousness limited to the skull or to one human being, or is consciousness a transcending aspect of Ultimate Reality in which man participates? If we define it in its broader context, then what you call intercessory prayer could be understood as the beneficial, loving radiance reaching out of one human consciousness for the welfare of another. We can say that indeed it is possible for one human being to reach his fellow man through his consciousness. This does not seem so mysterious if we think of others as being close by, perhaps in the same room. The presence of one loving individual can have a beneficial effect on others in the same room, even without his saying anything or doing anything. But the question is, Is this beneficial effect strong enough to reach to the next room, or across the street, or perhaps across the continent? Experience seems to indicate that it does. It seems that in the realm of the spirit, temporo-spatial coordinates and categories do not apply. Of course, human thinking finds it difficult to transcend the temporo-spatial categories because it is used to the idea of being limited spatially and temporally. But nevertheless, the more we understand that the nature of existence is spiritual consciousness, the more we see the value of liberating our mental potential from limiting categories such as agreement and disagreement. We also realize that love can liberate our minds from the categories of time and space, and thus we may discover the amazing potentialities for good that are within our reach.

*Comment:*   Concerning love and prayer for others, I wonder if it would be appropriate for me to repeat what I said after Dr. Hora's previous lectures. Someplace along the line, it hit me that Dr. Hora said that we should not confirm another person's self-pity—that this was not a function of a helpful relationship. For ten years or more I had listened periodically to one of my neighbors talk about the "ins and outs" of her children's involvements, her hostilities toward their teachers, how nobody was treating her family fairly, and so on. On the other hand, she is a wonderful person, a kindergarten teacher who has tremendous sensitivity for children, but this other half of her is just all mixed up. And so I listened and, as I said, I felt I deserved a halo for the patience and time I had been spending on her. So when Dr. Hora said that it is not helpful to sympathize with another person's self-pity, I suddenly thought, I don't think I have been doing this woman a service really, I have somehow got to change my attitude in listening to her. She hasn't called me since to weep on my shoulder! I have a different relationship with her now: we've exchanged gifts and we've talked pleasantries, we've discussed our mothers in a friendly way, but nothing is said about the damage that has been done to her and her family by others. This took place without special communication; I didn't tell her I had been to a conference and had come to a new insight.

The other thing in my recent experience that I think is related to being a beneficial presence has to do with one of our four children, who has had great difficulty in study and learning. In my busy household my mind was occupied with many things; the child was struggling at the dining room table. He had started on his work sheet and it was awful; he was just gazing out into space and nothing was happening. So I stopped what I was doing and sat down at the table and didn't say a word, but just sat there— I was with him. I have saved that piece of paper. The writing on the second half is completely different from the first. I didn't change it; I didn't say anything. On it is a note from the teacher that says, "Who did this?" Now you see, I know it happens but I don't know how, and I don't know how to repeat these things. Now this is what I would like to know, but I am afraid that's asking too much.

*Dr. Hora:* You remind me so much of a young mother who had considerable difficulties with her children and her husband. This woman went to see a psychiatrist to find out how to handle her family. She was told, "Look here, if the faucet in your kitchen is acting up, then you fix it, right? But if your children are acting up, you can't fix them. Somebody else has to fix them."

"That's why I am going to a psychiatrist," the mother replied.

"But the psychiatrist cannot fix them either. A psychiatrist is not a plumber of little children. Somebody else has to fix them."

"Well, who then?"

"Well, God has to fix them."

The patient exclaimed, "God! There is no God in our house."

But she learned that God could be invited into the house, provided she saw to it that the house had a loving climate. And this loving climate had to come through her consciousness, through her ways of thinking and viewing life. The first good thing that came of this was that she stopped trying to handle her children and her husband. Then she started to work it out with God, and one day she said, "You know, doctor, it works so well that I suspect it's a gimmick." In general, the tendency is to do something, to fix things, to objectify human existence. This naturally doesn't work; it only leads to complications.

*Question:*    Have you treated people who have tried to abandon the cigarette smoking habit by using the existential loving approach? And how have you been able to guide and help groups that might be having that kind of problem?

*Dr. Hora:*    Without having to deal with it directly, most patients tend to lose interest in it. This is how it happens: Cigarette smokers need cigarettes in order to keep themselves from being tense, restless, or in order to feel good, or in order to reward themselves for having felt good. The cigarette smoker smokes when he feels bad and he smokes when he feels good. No matter how he feels, he finds it necessary to smoke because he lives with his consciousness centered around the way he feels. Everybody takes it for granted that one ought to feel comfortable and it seems natural to want to feel comfortable. As a matter of fact, feeling comfortable is considered a sign of health. Feeling good and being healthy are intimately associated in our minds. Therefore, everyone is mostly concerned with feeling good, and some people seek good feelings one way and others another way. But this, of course, is an error, and the more we accept the assumption that feeling good is a proof of being healthy, the more we will be susceptible to using various kinds of auxiliary means for endeavoring to maintain a sense of well-being. The cigarette is the symbol and the means through which the smoker keeps confirming himself and his own sense of well-being. But when a patient enters into treatment, he discovers that feeling good is not synonymous with being healthy, even though being healthy doesn't mean that one feels bad. But as the mind becomes liberated from the overwhelming concern with its own well-being, it begins to lose interest in the various supportive means designed to assure its own well-being. To be healthy, man must be concerned with being good rather than with just feeling good. Now, this doesn't make much sense in the beginning, but when an individual can see that the quest for feeling good is really destructive to health, then he reaches the point of seeking another answer. He begins to understand that in order to feel good he has to be healthy first. To this end he must find the loving mode of being-in-the-world. Then he will lose interest in cigarette smoking, or in drinking, or in overeating, or in whatever he uses to confirm himself.

Many research projects are being conducted on cigarette smoking, with the aim of helping people to attack the problem directly, but this is difficult. For instance, in New York there is a large-scale undertaking designed to get people to stop smoking by telling them to affirm: "I choose not to smoke!" This seems to work with some people, but what does it really mean? It means that while previously they were using cigarette smoking to make themselves feel good, now they are trying to use a self-assertive slogan to make themselves feel good. Self-assertive slogans, however, may cause different troubles in life. So the solution really consists of shifting one's outlook on life or one's mode of being-in-the-world. Giving up one harmful habit for another may not be the best solution. Essentially, this is the existential answer to the problem of smoking.
*Comment:* It's interesting to find that what you've said explains more clearly to me why I was able on a certain day—May 22 of last year, to be exact—to stop smoking for good. I had tried to stop occasionally before by smoking less and not inhaling. I hadn't really taken it seriously. But one day I was reading an article in *The Friend* on the subject, and two things focused powerfully on the issue. We were at the time worked up about fallout, and in my mind I knew perfectly well that probably more people were being harmed by smoking than by fallout, and it was fundamentally insincere to march in front of the White House against nuclear testing while I continued this all-pervading habit. But that insight alone, I am sure, wouldn't have stopped me, for it was too widely humanitarian and tremendous. I also had a new granddaughter and I said to myself, her mother smokes an awful lot and this is very regrettable, but at least she wouldn't be able to say Granny smokes, too. And those two things did it.
*Dr. Hora:* Yes, at that time you decided that to be good is more important than to feel good.
*Comment:* Yes, but I have tried to be good before, from the point of view of being good. But the definition of goodness hadn't been sufficiently instinctive in its roots or wide enough in scope. I mean that this was both a wide spiritual concern for humanity, and also a deep, primitive concern for my own flesh and blood. And I think those two together were what did it.

*Dr. Hora:* Yes, in the literature that is called existential commitment. I like to call it an act of devotion.

*Comment:* How is her act being good? You haven't given us an example of what it is to be good. You have given us examples of trying to feel good. Was it because she fit it in with the experience of all humanity and her own life? Is it being good when you put yourself in that realm? Furthermore, being good has horrible implications for a good many of us.

*Dr. Hora:* Yes, we will have to elaborate on this. The word *good* was used only to put it in juxtaposition with feeling good. Feeling good versus being good. The emphasis is not so much on the "good" as on the "being"—feeling versus being. The cigarette smoker is guided by feeling. The existentially devoted individual sees life in terms of being. Let us not get stuck on the word *good* because—you are right—it is not enough to be good. More is needed. Our emphasis is on "being."

*Comment:* Couldn't you say that this example of giving up the cigarettes is similar to the example of inspiring the child to a better paper? When this spirit of love is available, there will be a loving response, and the important thing is having the radiation of that spirit of love—whether it is for the child with schoolwork, or for the child who is growing up and needs to be encouraged to have worthwhile goals instead of being dragged into the conformity of smoking. In other words, she was able to give up smoking partly because she recognized that this was one way of showing a greater love for her granddaughter.

*Dr. Hora:* That's right.

*Comment:* And it is the spirit of love that accomplishes it rather than pure self-assertiveness of the type that the newspapers are glorifying.

*Dr. Hora:* That's right. It is important to know the difference between an act of devotion and an act of self-will.

*Comment:* What about the Alcoholics Anonymous' belief that you can call on a power greater than yourself to give you the strength to withstand temptation. What is that? How would it be explained existentially? It seems to have been effective in many cases. Probably the reason it is effective is because those who hold it go out to be good to other people and to tell them what their experiences have been.

*Dr. Hora:* That's right.

*Comment:*   I think this is a very important part of overcoming the difficulty.

*Dr. Hora:*   Yes, there is a shift in concern here. The fundamental point is the shift of concern from feeling good to being a beneficial presence in the world.

# Dialogue VI

*Dr. Hora:* I've been doing some eavesdropping today on various groups. Strangely enough, many seemed very much taken by the idea of intercessory prayer. I don't know exactly what this means. Is it the loving heart that goes out to other people, or is it an aspect of psychotherapeutic zeal? Is there a desire to be able to do something to others by doing something for them? Now this seems like a subtle differentiation, yet an important one. We live in an age where techniques of manipulation of things and people are highly valued. However, to use prayer for manipulative purposes would be a fantastic distortion and sacrilege. Nevertheless, almost anything is conceivable. Of course, this would never really work. Perhaps the most important thing to realize here is that we cannot really manipulate people for their benefit. We can influence them only to their detriment. In a stricter sense, we cannot even influence ourselves for our benefit. Good can come only from a different source. It comes through us but not from us. And that's a good thing to know because the temptation to seek power over others or ourselves is very great. The results of this are, in the best case, always ambiguous—good and evil. Unequivocal good can come only from that source which is the only nondual reality.

*Comment:* Jesus said, *"Why callest thou me good? There is none good but one, that is God"* (Matt. 9:17).

*Dr. Hora:* Yes. Somebody addressed Jesus as "Good Master," and he pointed out that there is only one source of good: God. So he himself was not the source of good. He was a mediator of good, and we can be too. And that's where we come to intercessory prayer. When we want to benefit others, it stands to reason that first we have to know how to pray so as to benefit ourselves. This is the first task.

*Comment:* I thought that what we were doing in intercessory prayer was opening up a channel, not manipulating. Am I right?

*Question:* What do you mean "opening up a channel"?

*Answer:* Well, if I may be so bold, from God to the individual.

*Dr. Hora:* How do you do that?

*Comment:* Don't you have to open yourself in such a way that something can come through you? How can you pray for it to come to another person? Isn't this what is meant when we are challenged to becomes God's tools, God's witnesses?

*Dr. Hora:* Are you asking or are you answering this question?

*Comment:* I'm both asking and hypothesizing. To me this seems as though it could be an answer.

*Comment:* I thought when we pray for another person, that person becomes sensitive to—well, whatever you want to call it— God's power; therefore we are the channels for that person, are we not? I know when somebody is praying for me; he doesn't have to tell me.

*Comment:* Your caring helps strengthen the person for whom you are praying and also makes him want to be open to a receiving and a knowing.

*Question:* Dr. Hora, do I understand correctly that some of these expressions about the use of intercessory prayer come into the category that you would consider as not necessarily conveying an unequivocal good? I think I sensed that, but I may be wrong. If we feel that we are helpful, the person may feel helped, but aren't we manipulating?

*Comment:* Last September when a child was dying, I was asked to join two others in a hospital because the nurses said that prayer was the only thing that would save this child. I participated, and the child is now running around and walking and doing everything he should be doing, in spite of the fact that he was so close to death.

*Dr. Hora:* In order to understand this seemingly mysterious process, perhaps it would be advisable to go step by step and see whether we can expand our understanding by starting with those things that are easier to comprehend. As an illustration, let me present to you a riddle:

A little boy of eight was sent home from school with a note from the teacher stating that he had been unmanageable. He had been hitting little girls with his fist and had tripped his friend, with the disastrous result that the friend broke two front teeth. The mother of the boy was, naturally, quite upset and her first impulse was to devise a punishment that would really "teach the boy a lesson." The thought occurred to her that the most severe punishment she could inflict on him would be to take away his dog.

She consulted her psychiatrist, who told her to make sure she understood the meaning of the child's behavior before she took punitive action. When, however, no understanding was forthcoming, she was led to consider the meaning of her idea that the most severe punishment would be to deprive the child of his dog, his cherished possession. This seemed to indicate a belief that the worst thing that could happen to a person was to be separated from his cherished possession.

The mother admitted that indeed she was inclined to love rather possessively, and whenever she thought herself in danger of losing any of her cherished possessions, she tended to become belligerent, angry, and depressed. At this point the question arose whether perhaps the little boy, too, was in danger of losing something that he considered a cherished possession.

The mother said, "I cannot think of anything. As a matter of fact, my son was very happy because his grandparents were planning to stay in our house while my husband and I would be on vacation. Was the prospect of separation from us the problem? Of course, that must be the meaning of it! What should be done? Should we cancel our vacation and stay home?"

The psychiatrist replied, "If you cancel your vacation and stay home, you will confirm and gratify the child's possessive notion of love. If you go away, you will frustrate his possessive notion of love. In either case you will reinforce his possessive notion of love. It seems that right now, staying home would be no solution, nor would leaving help. You cannot punish the child, nor can you condone what he has done. You cannot blame yourself, nor are you without responsibility."

"What then is the solution?" asked the mother.

"That's a good question," answered the doctor.

Now suppose you put yourselves into the situation of this mother. The child needed to be healed of a problem, but he could not be healed directly.

*Question:* What about the mother?

*Dr. Hora:* Could the child be healed without the mother?

*Comment:* It is the family situation that must be healed.

*Dr. Hora:* The mother cannot go away and cannot stay home. What should she do?

*Comment:* It is rather surprising that she didn't think of it. It should be obvious that she should take the boy with her.

*Dr. Hora:* Let's bring in the consideration of intercessory prayer. If she would take him along, how would this solve the problem?

*Comment:* It wouldn't. It wouldn't help him grow up.

*Comment:* Couldn't she put a little bit of this into words to the child: "You are afraid of my going away, aren't you? I understand how you feel but . . . "

*Dr. Hora:* Unfortunately, words are of little help.

*Comment:* She could have sent him to the psychiatrist whom she was seeing. (laughter)

*Comment:* I think it is a long-term problem with the mother and the child, but taking the child with her might save somebody's teeth for a while.

*Comment:* The child wouldn't get better unless the mother got better.

*Comment:* All the solutions mentioned seemed to be forms of manipulation.

*Dr. Hora:* Right. Isn't it interesting that we tend to think in terms of manipulative solutions rather than healing or a resolution of the problem. Manipulation is an objectifying solution that tends to have aggravating consequences. *"For the good that I would, I do not: but the evil which I would not, that I do"* (Rom. 7:19). So the problem is that the child is imbued with a concept of possessiveness, and this concept, this idea of possessiveness, is reinforced both when it is gratified and when it is frustrated. Leaving for vacation would aggravate the possessive notion, staying home would also aggravate it, and taking him along would change nothing. As you see this is really a koan. You know what a koan is? A koan is a Zen riddle where you are in a bind whichever way you turn, yet there is a solution.

*Question:* Is this woman praying to be released from her own possessiveness?

*Comment:* It seems to me that the solution is not in going, staying, taking him, not taking him, but in establishing a greater sense of security in him, which she can do only by the giving of love. If this is possessive love then it is no help, but if it is the right kind of love that will give the child a sense of security, then it's from God.

*Dr. Hora:*   That's right. The child can only be healed by the healing of the mother. The mother must become a channel of love that
is not possessive but liberating. None of the other solutions are
real solutions except this one. Here we have a form of intercessory prayer where the healing of one individual is contingent on
the healing of another. It is good to realize that the mother could
talk to the child endlessly, and she could quote Drs. Spock and
Freud—or even Hora—and it wouldn't do any good at all, because what we say has no meaning unless it is fully expressive of
what we are. As long as the mother is inclined to love possessively,
the child is unable to love in any other way, and so the mother is
up against a wall. Parents constantly get into a bind because their
children force them to consider the issues of wholeness. Now how
does a mother, confronted with such an urgent situation, become
free of a lifelong habit of possessiveness?
*Comment:*   Sometimes it is not just lifelong, is it? It's an illness
that has been transmitted from one generation to another.
*Comment:*   When a child of mine was facing something like this,
I couldn't find any wholeness in myself and I ended up in the
church on my knees saying, "I give this child to you," but then I
looked at that crucifix and thought, "Will God treat him as he
treated his own son?" But the child found something in himself
that I had been keeping from him.
*Dr. Hora:*   Now you have touched on a very important point.
Doesn't that bring to mind the story of Abraham and Isaac?
Abraham reached the point of yielding his possessiveness of his
only son to such an extent that he was on the verge of surrender-
ing him totally to God (Gen. 22:1-14). Wasn't that really a
therapy of parental possessiveness? A parent has to come to a full
realization that his child is not his, but his child belongs to God,
that he always has belonged to God, and that he himself is but the
custodian. When the parent understands this truly, he loves without possessiveness. A released child can then grow freely and
without anxiety at points of separation. Separation anxiety, which
is generally believed to be a serious problem, disappears at the
point of realization that there is no separation. We are always living and moving and having our being in God. However, until such
time as parents understand this and gain a sense of peace concerning their children, the children cannot be helped.
    Now let us consider the following: If the mother is at home, the
quality of her presence is transmitted to the child directly, and the

child can sense whether he is being loved possessively or freely. Here the mother is in immediate contact with the child. The intercessory prayer is active as direct communication. Now suppose the mother has to go away. Can she continue her healing of the child at a distance? Many of you are nodding more or less in agreement. Some are uncommitted, but some are nodding. Apparently, you think that this is possible.

*Comment:* She is working on herself.

*Dr. Hora:* Right!

*Comment:* She can do that just as well on the boat as at home, perhaps even better.

*Dr. Hora:* Possibly. We see, however, that when it comes to intercessory prayer, the primary factor is the individual himself. His harmony with God makes him a channel. A channel receives and manifests or transmits that which it has received, but it doesn't operate or manipulate what it has received. It doesn't do anything. This is entirely an issue of consciousness. Many people find this very frustrating, and they ask, "How can you do something without doing anything?" This is a Taoistic concept—called the "action that is nonaction." In other words, when we think of accomplishing something, we immediately conjure up a certain activity in our minds. It is hard for us to conceive of action that is not activity, a condition that is neither active nor passive, yet efficacious. Whoever would want to be a healing factor in the life of another must work on himself.

*Comment:* When my daughter was about eight, she suffered terribly from a possessive, domineering mother. She was then vacationing on a farm in the mountains in Switzerland, and I went to visit her. The moment I arrived, she immediately assumed an attitude of resisting everything. In deep desperation over the situation, after all the children had gone to bed, I walked up and down the mountain path and just said over and over again, "You be you and I'll be me. You be you and I'll be me," and I said this until I was tired of it. I went to bed and the next morning her mood was entirely different and she was agreeable and amenable and we could talk. I wish I could say it lasted. We took her to the village and bought her some needlework, which she wanted, and when she got back and started to embroider this thing, I began making suggestions. It was right back the way it had been before, but I never forgot it because it was really like a miracle.

*Comment:* I think there are several people here who remember Harvey Haines. He was a Friend at Montclair Meeting, and not only at Meeting but in other small groups, Harvey Haines had a certain wholeness. When he came into a room, the quality of the silence was changed. He didn't have to say anything. He didn't have to do anything; he just was and that's about it.

*Question:* Dr. Hora, can't the child sometimes free the mother by refusing to be possessed?

*Dr. Hora:* The child frees the mother by driving her to desperation.

*Comment:* How about the father?

*Comment:* The father is out playing golf . . .

*Dr. Hora:* The same goes for the father, naturally.

*Comment:* It seems to me we glide over possessiveness as something someone can pick up or take off. This problem of possessiveness in mothers is very deep-rooted and, contrary to what the other lady says, it takes many, many hours on the couch.

*Dr. Hora:* Please, do not get stuck on the problem of possessiveness. It is not the subject of our concern. We are talking about intercessory prayer. He who would heal another, let him be healed first himself. This is the primary and essential factor in intercessory prayer. We have to be concerned about the quality of our presence. What determines the quality of our presence?

*Comment:* How much ego has been eliminated.

*Comment:* How much love is one able to give others. How loving one is. Our degree of wholeness.

*Dr. Hora:* Certainly. What determines that?

*Question:* Presence in respect to what? Merely existing?

*Dr. Hora:* Presence with respect to the present.

*Question:* What is presence?

*Comment:* How helpfully a person is really there. How much of him is there.

*Comment:* It has something to do with the quality of his consciousness.

*Dr. Hora:* That's right. Can somebody explain what it is we are talking about when we say an individual has a certain quality of presence?

*Comment:* Is it not an individual who brings to others the idea of truth and of love? He may not necessarily know it himself. He doesn't have to do that, but the quality of his presence as an individual makes the others realize a truer conception of the love of God and of fellow man.

*Dr. Hora:* You have described an individual whose quality of presence is particularly satisfying and comforting.

*Comment:* Not only that, but in whose presence one felt that somehow one was more than one was really meant to be. You felt more truly yourself when Harvey Haines was in the room. We all knew him and our little pettinesses disappeared.

*Dr. Hora:* Would you want to explain his secret?

*Comment:* Well, you asked for a definition of presence. I think when we say the word *presence* we are saying that we are important to one another and that we really matter. I mean what kind of feelings or ideas or reactions we generate in each other. Something is always going on.

*Dr. Hora:* Some people's presence is an absent one and some people's presence is an obtrusive one, an overbearing one, or a joyous one, or an exciting one, or a seductive one, or an inspiring one, or an illuminating one, or a healing one. There are infinite shadings of qualities of presence. Now, our destiny depends on the quality of our presence because this is what people respond to. This is the key that either opens the door of opportunity and advancement and the good in life—or shuts it. There are some people who never seem to have any difficulties. Wherever they go, everything seems to open for them and they don't know strain; the burdens of life are light to them. Jesus said, *"Take my yoke upon you . . . for my yoke is easy, and my burden is light"* (Matt. 12:29-30). What is this yoke? This yoke that makes burdens seem light? It is the quality of presence, and it is contingent, as you said, on our consciousness. Now what determines the state of our consciousness?

*Comment:* It seems to me that if we are conscious of God in us, that God is in all life and therefore is in us, in our consciousness, and if it's in our consciousness other people can't help but see it, more or less.

*Comment:* Our consciousness is the result of the predominating thought that we indulge in and the way in which we direct our thought.

*Dr. Hora:* Yes, our thoughts determine our consciousness. Now what determines our thoughts?

*Comment:* Many things. I don't understand it. We could think about God, but our thought can't produce God.

*Dr. Hora:* Right. Now we all have our heads full of thoughts all the time. Right? Maybe we would like it not to be so, but it is so. Where do these thoughts come from?

*Comment:*  They come from above.

*Comment:*  I wish they did.

*Comment:*  Well, Jesus said, Love God with all your faculties of expression—heart, soul, strength, mind, and so on. From this relationship come thoughts and rich experiences.

*Question:*  Do thoughts come from body, mind and spirit? And can we will our consciousness to dwell on them, more or less?

*Dr. Hora:*  You are close. Any other suggestions?

*Comment:*  They come from desires. That's what I understood you to say—that they come from desires.

*Dr. Hora:*  Well, desires are thoughts. . . . Where do thoughts come from? What determines our thoughts?

*Comment:*  Our concerns.

*Dr. Hora:*  In other words, our perspective on life determines our thoughts.

*Comment:*  I am confused when you speak about thoughts.

*Dr. Hora:*  The Bible says: *"Where your treasure is there will your heart be also"* (Matt. 6:21). What does that mean? Our mental orientation determines the thoughts we entertain. This is important because that's how it happens that Freudians have Freudian thoughts, Jungians have Jungian thoughts, etc. In order that our quality of presence be a wholesome one, our thoughts need to be Godly. How do they become Godly? By walking around with the Bible? No. How, then, can our consciousness be under continuous impact of Godly thoughts?

*Question:*  Would not loving—being loving—be the way?

*Dr. Hora:*  Yes.

*Comment:*  Not literal prayer, in the conventional sense of the word.

*Dr. Hora:*  Right.

*Comment:*  Prayer of being—if you love life—is the same as having faith in life . . .

*Dr. Hora:*  Is it clear what existential worship is? Existential worship assures you the broadest possible perspective that a human being can have—the perspective of love. The loving outlook on life has as its central concern to be and to live lovingly—being loving under all circumstances, as far as it is within our power. If this is our central devotion, then our consciousness is constantly flooded with such thoughts as result in a beneficial quality of presence, and thus we are continuously inspired by creative ideas.

# Identity

In connection with the attainment of wholeness, the following question is sometimes asked: "Why don't you tell us how to do it?" However, if the question is phrased this way, we are off on a wrong tangent, for wholeness cannot be done. There are two common pitfalls in this sphere: thinking in terms of cause and effect, and thinking in terms of techniques. Techniques may be generally useful, but in the realm of being they are not applicable. In addition to thinking in terms of doing, there is also the tendency to think in terms of having. This is an additional stumbling block, for what we have and what we do is not what we are. To know what we are is perhaps the most important issue of life.[6]

The Zen Buddhists have a koan: "There is a goose in a bottle. How does the goose get out of the bottle?" Every time the student comes up with a conceptual answer, he gets rejected. In other words, he is required to give the answer with the totality of his being. In a sense we could view life as a charade requiring us to express the truth of being, not in words, not with activities, not in symbols, but with the quality of our presence. As long as we do not express the truth of being, we are just like a goose in a bottle: squeezed in a mold. A goose in a bottle cannot grow, it cannot develop its potential and it tends to wonder forever how it would feel to be another goose in another bottle. In order for the goose to be liberated, it would have to become consciously that which it really is. The knowledge of the truth of being makes us free.

To begin with, we must refuse to think of ourselves and of others in terms of what we do or what we have. Suppose somebody has a diploma. We call him a doctor. Does this make him really a doctor? No, he has a doctorate. Somebody may have a Cadillac.

Does that determine his being? Somebody may have money. Does
that determine his being? No. It may determine his social comforts
and other things, but not his being.

A patient said to his psychiatrist, "If I had two million dollars,
I wouldn't need you." The doctor, puzzled, asked him why he
thought of two million. The patient replied, "Because one million
I have, but it doesn't do me any good." We may further ask: We
have a body, but are we our body? We have a gender, but are we
our gender? We have emotions, but are we our emotions? We
have sensations, but are we our sensations? We have thoughts, but
are we our thoughts? Whatever we have, that's not what we are.
If we are none of these things, what are we then? And where are
we? Is this important? I think it is.

Many of you have, no doubt, seen the Zen pictures called Ox
Herding. These represent an attempt at pictorial guidance toward
the realization of the truth of being. I will describe these pictures
in succession: In the first picture, a man in a thicket of brush,
walking around lost in ignorance, confusion, directionless, at the
mercy of the elements; in short, a completely unenlightened, even
unself-conscious man. In the next picture he discovers the foot-
prints of a bull and begins to follow them. In the third picture, he
sees the bull and runs after it. In the following picture, he has
caught the bull and he struggles with it. In the next picture he
leads the bull home by a rope. In the sixth picture, he rides on the
bull triumphantly. In the following picture, he sits alone and con-
templates the world. He realizes that there never was a bull. The
ninth picture is completely empty. He realizes that there is neither
bull nor self. There is emptiness, which means that at this point
he discovers that whatever he has and whatever he does, that's not
what he really is. The last picture is called "In the World." Here
we see him in the company of another man. The commentary
says: "I live among people just like anybody else, except wherever
I go even the dead trees come alive." Now what does this mean?
Doesn't it mean that his presence in the world has become a beneficial one? Jesus was a great example of a beneficial presence. It
is described, for instance, that when he met a funeral he went over
to the bier and said, *"Young man I say unto thee arise"* (Lk. 7:14),
and the dead boy came alive. Wherever he went, people were
healed and sinners reformed without his doing anything in particular. Jesus didn't do anything. He just was. It was the quality
of his presence that made the dead come to life. This is the great

attainment—to know the truth of being. Interestingly enough, the truth is there whether we know it or not. However, it is demanded of us that we aspire to know it. We must seek to know it consciously, otherwise we are lost and floundering in the thicket.

Now we may ask: What is the meaning of the bull? In this connection, let us consider the following discussion about the problem of anger. Somebody said, "One should get angry, it's supposedly good for us." Somebody else said, "One should get angry slowly." Then someone else said, "We should control our anger." In turn, a young lady said, "I once hit my husband over the head with a sausage and ever since then things have gone much better in our marriage." Someone else countered, "We should never get angry." Somebody retorted, "Then you'll get sick." Now it seems that these friends were wrestling with a "bull." We all do until we reach the point where we can truly know that there never really was a "bull," that the "bull" has no reality. Granted that this point is not easily reached, but it can be. A man driving on Riverside Drive in New York City was stopped by an elderly lady who asked, "Which way are you driving?" The driver replied, "I am going south on the Henry Hudson Parkway," and the lady shouted, "Then drop dead!" Did the driver get angry? He could have. He could have told her off, but he knew that there was no "bull," that he didn't have to get angry. His blood pressure was in no way affected. Whatever seems to be real and is not, is the "bull." Fear is a "bull," too. Who is free of fear? The one who is free of anger, who knows the unreality of the "bull." Do we not wrestle with fear? Do we not try to overcome fear? Do we not try to control fear and tame it so we can ride on it? Whoever believes in taking courage is a fighter against the "bull" of fear. And if he is very courageous, he can ride on the "bull," but he is still involved with it. Now it is possible to reach a point of understanding where we can know that there is no "bull." And how do we reach that point? The Bible has a very simple prescription for it: *"There is no fear in love; but perfect love casteth out fear"* (1 Jn. 4:18). A well-known story illustrates this point beautifully. It goes like this: Fear knocked on the door. Love answered, "There is no one here."

Interestingly enough, the Buddhists don't put it this way. They say you have to discover emptiness and then you will know that there is no fear, no anger, no pride, no vanity, no envy, no jealousy, no materialism nor mad ambition.[7] To reach emptiness seems

difficult to us because it strikes us somewhat as being told to re-
move darkness from a room. This can best be done by introduc-
ing the light. Therefore, the biblical recommendation seems to
work better for us. To paraphrase: Perfect love casteth out all
"bulls." The love of being loving brings us into harmony with
Existence and reveals the truth of all things.

# Dialogue VII

*Question:* Isn't there a danger of making a "bull" out of love?

*Dr. Hora:* Is it possible to make a "bull" out of love?

*Comment:* Surely not true love.

*Dr. Hora:* Love is the harmonizing, liberating principle of Existence. Of course, nobody is free of the educational process of having had to wrestle with the "bull" before he was able to realize that the whole thing wasn't really necessary.

*Question:* Are all ten pictures necessary, or can their sequence be broken at any point?

*Dr. Hora:* It would seem that everybody must go through the whole process. Such is the human condition. This is really what is meant by having to be born again.

*Question:* Well, if you think there is no "bull" to wrestle with, are you just fooling yourself?

*Dr. Hora:* Right. You have to know it.

*Comment:* By wrestling?

*Dr. Hora:* By having reached the realization of it. You can come to know it in the course of living.

*Comment:* Could you expand on the idea of the intellect and reason as a "bull"?

*Dr. Hora:* Just as emotion can be a "bull," the intellect can be a "bull," and sensuousness can be a "bull." As we said before, some people are fixated on sensuality, some on emotionality, some on intellectuality, and some on all three. The interesting thing is that the "bull" seems increasingly real as we fight against it. Someone may ask, why not ignore the "bull?" However, if we ignore it, the "bull" would gore us. And someone may ask, why not kill the "bull?" That would be suicide because we identify ourselves with our "bull"; we think the "bull" is part of us. We cannot kill the "bull"; we cannot run from the "bull"; we cannot fight the "bull."

*Comment:* You accept the "bull."

*Dr. Hora:* When you accept the "bull," you make reality out of unreality.

*Comment:*   I notice that you have coined a new phrase: "the love of being loving."

*Dr. Hora:*   Yes, it is good that you brought it up. With this concept we can improve our traditional way of thinking. This helps us to transcend the subject/object dichotomy. When we say we love God, our minds immediately insert a wall between man and God. There is a separation here and we establish a "self and other" situation, which is called the subject/object dichotomy, or split. However, if we get accustomed to thinking in terms of "the love of being loving," then we have overcome the separation between God and man and that is very helpful. If you love being loving, you dwell in love and *"he that dwelleth in love dwelleth in God and God in him"* (1 Jn. 4:16). Here there is no dichotomy between subject and object. For God is not an object and neither is he a subject.

*Comment:*   He is omnipresent.

*Dr. Hora:*   He is All in All.

# The Epistemology of Love

It is strange that under ordinary circumstances man seldom talks in order to really say something; neither does he remain silent in such a way as to say nothing. Ordinarily, when man talks he is mostly concerned with making himself feel good. And when he keeps quiet he is not really quiet; he talks to himself silently. His mind dwells not so much on the truth of what really is, as on manifold ways and means of making himself feel good and of avoiding feeling bad.

The preoccupation with feeling good, secure, strong, influential, and successful isolates man's consciousness from reality and hampers his cognitive and responsive faculties. Man derives pleasurable or comforting experiences and sensations from the gratification of his assumptions. Assumptions are thoughts of "what should be." When the "should be" is gratified, reality is ignored. Man tends to live to a greater or lesser degree in a private world of illusions. He is thus more or less estranged, alienated, and disconnected from life, reality, truth, love.

Man who is concerned with feeling good spends most of his life in "pursuit of happiness" and thus tends to miss out on truth, reality, love, communion, joy, health. For while illness is "disease" and health is "ease," ease is not necessarily health. The pursuit of ease does not lead to health. The pursuit of happiness, of feeling good, of being successful, as ends in themselves, is mostly self-defeating; these are at best only by-products of the loving mode of being-in-the-world. For instance, the quest for sexual pleasure and successful "performance" produces mutual exploitation with interpersonal complications that often result in such disorders as impotency and frigidity.

The concern with feeling good makes man a hedonist. He tends to become a "consumer" of cigarettes, alcohol, chewing gum, candy, drugs. To him, things become means to an end. People, business, profession, children, friends, objects, ideas, religion, and education all become tools and gimmicks serving the purpose of making him feel good. The hedonistic view of life tends to produce severe forms of egotism and a progressive deterioration of cognitive and responsive faculties.

The striving to feel good is the foundation of ambitions, competitiveness, success-hunting, pleasure- and power-seeking. The primary concern with feeling good is a misguided mode of being-in-the-world. It makes man unavailable to the cognitive faculty that constitutes the prerequisite for love.

Love is essentially a mode of cognition. Love is concerned neither with feeling good nor with feeling bad. Love is concerned with understanding. Love listens to hear. Love is a state of complete attention, without intruding thoughts and motivations. Contrary to general belief, love is not just a feeling or emotion. The opposite of love is not hate, as is generally assumed. The opposite of love is calculative thinking (in the sense of Heidegger's "das vorstellende Denken"). The opposite of thinking is not non-thinking; it is paying attention to understand.

The term *paying attention* is of some semantic significance because it implies a certain sacrifice or payment or giving up of something. The question offers itself: What is the payment that is being paid in paying attention? The payment in paying attention is the giving up or sacrificing of a certain mental content. This means that to pay attention one must give up certain thoughts and cherished assumptions. The mental currency to be paid for attention is the giving up or letting go of favorite assumptions. Mental assumptions are the price to be paid for the realization of the loving state of consciousness.

Attention is a state of mental receptivity to whatever is, in contradistinction to concentration and fascination, which are object-oriented selective states of cognitive focusing. The object of attention is understanding. The object of love is Love. Love is that intelligence which forever reveals itself as Understanding. The concern with feeling good ignores love. Ignorance is that mental activity which ignores what is forever available. Ignorance then is not a passive state. Neither is love. Love is neither active nor passive. In order for love to come into being, both activity and passivity must "die."

*"Whosoever would lose his life for my sake, shall find it"* (Lk. 9:24). This well-known utterance of Jesus is of great significance for existential psychology. "For my sake" means for the sake of love. To lose one's life means to abandon the false meanings of life, to drop the misguided endeavors and concerns that give the illusion of constituting the essence of life. After a relatively short time in psychotherapy one patient remarked: "I don't understand how it happened but I lost my fear of dying. I never spoke to you about it but it used to be my most pressing problem." Actually, what happened was that the patient shifted her concern from the gratification of a desire for power and dominance to a realization of the essential significance of the loving mode of existence. This revealed to her that the fear of dying was the fear of discovering that what had previously seemed all-important in her life was based on erroneous assumptions.

Commitment to love is often experienced as frightening. Actually, love requires man to let go of all attachments, outward and inward. More often than not it seems particularly difficult to loosen the hold on mental attachments, for this amounts to what could be called "losing one's mind," because what is considered to be mind consists of memories and learned knowledge, assumed notions, favorite strivings. All this must be out of the way for understanding to occur. Since love is complete attention, it must be undivided. The striving, clutching, ambitious man is incapable of undivided attention; his consciousness is impaired, his cognition is deficient, his contact with reality tenuous. Such a man exists on an abased level of mentality. Love is that state of consciousness which brings human potentialities to optimal degrees of realization.

Pleasure-seeking man's consciousness is focused on gratification. Desires, if gratified, tend to increase; if frustrated, they tend to become more urgently demanding. As long as there is desire and "pursuit of happiness" in any form, there is anxiety, suffering and conflict. Love is neither gratification nor frustration. Love is harmony with what really is. It is at-one-ment with the flux of life.

Just as ignorance is an active ignoring of what is, anxiety is in no sense something that, so to speak, befalls man. It is self-manufactured. Anxiety is that disturbance of consciousness which is caused by the discrepancy between what "should be" and what really is. Anxiety is generated by the ignoring of the actual. It is the experiential awareness of pursuing a false reality.

Freedom from anxiety and freedom from ignorance are contingent on the same condition, namely, on the cognitive harmony with what is. This, in turn, can only take place in the absence of mental presuppositions concerning what "should be." Fear, then is a product of thought and so is everything else outside of love. True love cannot be thought. Love that is thought is not love; it is a concept, an idea about love. True love can be neither given nor gotten. When it is, it gives itself. True love can only be lived as a state of consciousness.

## LOVE AND SELF

The seat of anxiety, fear, pleasure, and pain is in that conceptual system called the self or the ego. Without the self, fear has no place to be.

The mind that is attached to the object world—or to the world of ideas and concepts, or to self and others—does not dwell in the realm of Understanding, that is, in the realm of Love. It dwells in the realm of assumptions.

The sphere of the interpersonal is the interrelationship of two conceptual systems, so-called self systems. Conceptual systems are unreal in themselves. In the interpersonal sphere of consciousness there is no understanding of what really is. There is only mental manipulation and calculative thought.

Discordant conditions are evidence of the fact that consciousness has left the realm of Love and become attached to the abstract, alien self. Love is that background of harmony which is obscured but also revealed by the foreground of the discordant ego. The Japanese term *Yugem* points to that cognitive phenomenon in which the background is meaningfully highlighted by the foreground.

*"All things work together for good"* (Rom. 8:28) for those who dwell in a loving state of consciousness. A man who understands love becomes immune to hate, intolerance, and sensory attachments. To love "Unattached in the Tao" means to understand love as the "essence and destiny of All Things." Love heals. It makes man whole by enabling him to transcend the dualities and multiplicities of the phenomenal world.

There is an apparent dialectic tension between the self and love. Man is turned either toward love or toward self. In the final analysis there is really no other choice.

In dreams, beliefs, assumptions, and thoughts tend to become images. During waking hours thoughts and assumptions tend to become actions, behavior, bodily experiences, and even structural changes, that is, diseases of the body, mind, feelings, and behavior.

Lovelessness inevitably leads to psychological, somatic, or social complications; discord; and illness. When confronted with his self-generated problems, man tends to fall into the error of attempting to cure himself by "figuring out" the reasons for his suffering and then devising methods to change himself. All such intentions, efforts, and attempts are naive and self-righteous. They ignore the real source of healing that is the outcome of the realization of Love-Intelligence-Understanding as a state of consciousness and a mode of existence.

The subjective perspective on life is a source of suffering. The objective perspective is subjective. Truth is neither objective nor subjective; it is transcendent.

Self-centered consciousness does not discern love as the Ground of Being. Interpersonal consciousness is focused on the interaction of the self and the other; it also fails to see that background without which a foreground could not appear. The interpersonal focus ignores the truth of what really is, because it is concerned with the relationship of the self to the other. It does not realize that the self is the same as the other, since the other is but an other self. In the realm of Understanding there is neither "self " nor "other"; there is only that which really is.

Loveless man often manifests "nervous tension," which is essentially hunger for gratification of wrong desires. The slave of wrong desires suffers when gratified and suffers when not gratified. Wrong desires hurt. The gratification of wrong desires leaves an unpleasant aftertaste. Desire desires the gratification of the self. Man too often prefers to glorify himself rather than to love.

Wrong desires can only be displaced by one desire, that is, concern, and that is love. Love frees the mind of wrong desires. When the concern with love takes precedence over all desires, there is a change of base—a reorientation toward that which brings harmony into man's life. The experiential realization that there is no fear in love suffices for a complete commitment to a loving mode of being-in-the-world.

The self, however, is forever seeking to attract consciousness to itself and thus divert it from truth. Man is inclined to concentrate on the self or on the "other"—the body, clothes, behavior, feelings, appearances—and thus loses contact with that which is accessible to the loving mode of cognition. Love is complete attention to what really is.

Fear and anxiety are experiential evidences of not seeing the actual. Moreover, they further distract attention by attracting it to themselves, and thus a vicious cycle is established. Fear is never of what really is, but of what one *thinks* is. Man is frightened by his assumptions—assumptions that originate mostly in childhood experiences and are exaggerated by the helplessness of the child's perspective in relationship to the adult world.

Defensive concerns hamper and deflect consciousness from the task of cognizing what is. Defensive man is preoccupied with what should be, namely, the security and gratification of the self. Or he is preoccupied with what should not be, namely, anxiety, fear, and discomfort.

## LOVE AND TIME

Thought as memory is of the past. Anxiety is a product of thought. The habit of thought interferes with cognition and produces disturbances of consciousness. The past as anticipated future obscures the reality of the present.

Anticipatory anxieties are fears of assumptions, that is, the fear of the past repeating itself in the future. Love precludes fear and anxiety because it is fully observed in the seeing of what really is in the present. Love is not concerned with self or other, with feeling good or bad, with being safe or unsafe, with self-esteem or humiliation, with recognition or ridicule. It is concerned only with understanding and responding. It is, then, vital to learn the open-minded confrontation of what really is. Such a confrontation leads to a liberation of the mind from assumptions. This can only be from moment to moment. It means responding to life, not on the basis of past experiences, but rather on the strength of one's cognitive resources available at all times.

*"That which hath been is now; and that which is to be hath already been; and God requireth that which is past"* (Eccl. 3:15). Love requires man to let go of the past. The loving mode of cognition can only come into being when consciousness is emptied of memory traces, assumptions, and strivings. Truth cannot be cognized purely on the basis of past experiences. What is required is an unequivocal commitment to understanding of what takes place from moment to moment. When light enters, darkness vanishes. Light dissipates darkness. The truth of what really is dissolves preconceptions.

Knowledge is always of the past. Discursive knowledge is not unlike belief. Belief is that mental content which provides man with an illusory sense of security. Man is eager to have his beliefs confirmed and dreads having them challenged. As long as there are beliefs there is anxiety.

The child who is afraid of the dark and the adult who is afraid to be alone are frightened not by what really is, but by their thoughts about what might be. Their fear is due to thinking, imagining, expecting. However, man can only think that which was; he cannot think what is or what shall be. So man is afraid only of the past. The past, however, has no reality, as it is memory. Therefore, fear has no reality; fear is a product of thought.

Cognition of the present is entrance into the realm of love. Only love can free the mind of the past with its prevalently childish assumptions, memories, and misinterpretations. Love is that state of consciousness which is capable of cognizing the truth. Truth liberates from bondage to assumptions.

The self, too, is the past. The self ignores the present. In seeing what is, the self and the past are not. There is neither thinking nor fear in the present. In the present there is only responding to that which reveals itself from moment to moment.

## LIBERATION

That which is clung to is defended. That which is desired is clung to. That which is desired and clung to is cherished. If truth and love are cherished, nothing is clung to—and man is free. Liberation is the realization of that cognitive freedom which is true love. It can be attained by learning the meaning of letting-be, of meditation, mind-fasting, encounter, and cognitive transcendence.

1. *Letting-be* (not to be confused with leaving alone) is that mode of being that is characterized by reverent, choiceless awareness of what is in order that it may reveal itself in the essence of its being. It is that mental attitude which facilitates understanding. Letting-be opens the mind to unimpeded cognition.

2. *Meditation* is the practice of mindfulness (awareness) of the past interfering with the present in the form of assumptions, beliefs, desires, marginal thoughts. Meditation transcends time.

3. *Mind-fasting* is a method of bringing the mind into focus with the Infinite through awareness (that is, experiential understanding) of the self as being merely conceptual in character. The mind that is focused on the Infinite (indefinite) is in a state of undivided attention. Undivided attention is capable of seeing whatever reveals itself in its full and proper context. Mind-fasting transcends the self.

4. *Encounter* is the crucible of existential psychotherapy. The full import and reality of love is best revealed when, as a result of a series of meaningful encounters with a loving, understanding being, a healing experience comes about. Love makes whole. Encounter transcends the subject/object dichotomy.

5. *Cognitive transcendence* is a supreme state of intelligence that "sees through" all mental, physical, and interpersonal phenomena that would tend to obscure the luminous lucidity of love in man's consciousness. Truth is not visible, yet it is clearly seen.

# Commentary on a Lecture
# at a Scientific Meeting

Dr. Charles Hulbeck's rich and inspired paper, "On Creative Phases in Psychoanalysis," seems to contain five points of significance. In the beginning we are given an unusual but rather portentous definition of growth. Growth, says Dr. Hulbeck, is the ability "to see the deeper realities of life, though they are covered up and distorted." We venture to assume that Dr. Hulbeck begins his paper with an implied therapeutic credo, namely, the desirability of developing one's capacities to cognize the deeper realities of life. Thus, psychotherapy can be rightfully considered a process of cognitive unfoldment.

The intimate relationship between cognition and creativity is rather self-evident. As a matter of fact, creativity can be thought of as consisting of a cognitive and an executive phase. We could point out here the marvelous way in which language reveals the meaning of creativity by saying that the creative individual realizes what he has realized. That is, he gives formal expression to what he has come to understand, perceive, cognize. And so we can say that Dr. Hulbeck, in his paper, endeavors to demonstrate to us the stages of the analytic process where the cognitive realizations of the therapeutic encounter are transformed first into dialogic realizations, then into existential realization.

In his second point Dr. Hulbeck deals with the phenomenology of the encounter, which he describes as a "collision of two different worlds." To those unfamiliar with the dramatic language of existential philosophers this may sound somewhat jarring. However, what is undoubtedly meant here is the fact that in the encounter the patient is afforded an opportunity to discover a multitude of tacit assumptions that he may have been taking for granted, never realizing to what extent they were determining his life experience.

The question may arise here as to how it is that the therapeutic encounter can provide a patient with such illuminating discoveries? In this connection, Dr. Hulbeck alludes to a phenomenon that he calls the "creative vacuum," and the necessary ability of the analyst to experience it. This may well be one of the most important postulates of existential analysis, for this is the point of phenomenological perception where truth reveals itself to the unprejudiced mind. Heidegger makes this the central issue of his work *Sein und Zeit,* saying: "Nothingness in contrast to all that is, is the veil of Being."

It may be useful to reiterate here that without the capacity for the phenomenological mode of cognition, existential analysis is beyond the reach of the average scientifically trained individual. Moreover, it often strikes him as absurd and rather an irritating nuisance. Therefore, he is often inclined to dismiss it as mystical nonsense.

We can say, then, that the therapeutic encounter is a creative situation by virtue of the therapist's phenomenological mode of participation in it, in contrast to the traditional technical and discursively interpretative one.

Out of the tensions of nothingness emerge the creative revelations of the truth of what is from moment to moment. This, in turn, requires elucidation with the aid of the dialogue, which is Dr. Hulbeck's third point: "In contrast (to other dialogues), the analytical dialogue originates from silence."

This dialogue eventually leads to shedding light upon the patient's mode of being-in-the-world, which if I am not mistaken, Dr. Hulbeck calls "the articulation process." This would be Dr. Hulbeck's fourth point. Closely tied in with it is his fifth point, called the "primary choice." It seems fair to assume that primary choice means a subjectively all-important concern to which a patient is knowingly or unknowingly committed and that determines his particular articulation with existence. That is, an individual's primary choice constitutes his orientation in life and largely determines his mode of being-in-the-world.

Dr. Hulbeck has chosen to conclude his scholarly presentation by a quote from Maimonides: "If I were not interested in myself, what would others be able to do for me, and if I were not interested in myself, what would I be able to do for others?" Maimonides was no doubt a great physician and philosopher; however, this particular quotation seems to recommend self-concern as a primary choice. In existential terms it might be preferable to say the following: "If patients were not interested in the truth of being, what would anyone be able to do for them, and if psychiatrists were not interested in the truth of being, what would they be able to really do for anyone?" And without man's abiding quest for ultimate reality, would there be any progress at all?

*Essay Eleven*

# Religious Values
# in Illness and Health

One of the significant characteristics of man is that he is somehow impelled to be constantly concerned with the preservation,
unfolding, and fulfillment of existence. Throughout his life, therefore, man is in search of ideas that would enable him to fulfill this
compelling necessity. Thus, certain ideas tend to become invested
with greater importance because they are believed to be life-enhancing. These ideas, beliefs, convictions, then, become existential concerns.

In general, it is possible to distinguish three major categories of
concerns that man commits himself to. The most primitive of
these is the striving to secure the fulfillment of existence through
the concern with having. Having can become an all-pervasive
mental preoccupation extending over a wide range of possibilities—from having material objects to having living things, from
having and possessing people to having a personality, from having sensations and emotions (which can be either painful or pleasurable) to having knowledge, status, influence, connections, all
the way to "having religion."

The second, somewhat more advanced, view of life is centered
in the concern with doing, being able to do, to function. Individuals holding this view seek the fulfillment of life in activities, pro-
ductiveness, performance, capabilities, techniques, sexual prow-
ess, religious rituals and practices.

The third commitment is found in individuals who, having
understood the meaning of man as the "image and likeness of
God," are dedicated to the concern with being. This means that
they endeavor to center their existence around the expression of
love, truth, mercy, justice, understanding, wholesomeness. They

109

have come to understand that the two previous aspects of human experience, namely having and doing, can be meaningful only if they are consequences of the authentic mode of being-in-the-world and not primary attainments.

The phenomenological elucidation of having, doing, and being as three modes of being-in-the-world greatly contributes to our understanding of some of the most baffling syndromes of pathological religiosity in their various modalities and intensities, from the so-called normal to the clinically bizarre. As a matter of fact, the existential perspective on being shows certain pathological entities that have hitherto been considered extremely complex to be much simpler. The existential perspective has revealed these pathological entities to be various manifestations and consequences of misdirected modes of being-in-the-world.

For instance, a teenager, the son of orthodox Jewish parents, who in school was considered brilliant, especially in science and mathematics, quite suddenly became very much interested in listening to religious programs on radio and television. The Bible became his inseparable companion. One day he confronted his parents with a surprise announcement that he had been baptized and henceforth would live as a Christian. The parents were very much distressed by this and unable to understand what had happened. When they subsequently caught him displaying his genitals to his sister, they took him to Bellevue for psychiatric observation. From Bellevue the patient was transferred to a state hospital. When seen in conference there, he was clutching his Bible and some notes containing mathematical formulas. In conversation he revealed considerable intellectual brilliance and an impressive capacity to quote from the Bible in a coherent and meaningful way. However, one thing stood out very clearly: he "possessed" his knowledge. He "had" it all to himself, in his head and in his book. Religion and knowledge were "his possessions," which no one else in the family had or could take from him; he thought his parents and the doctors would be inclined to do so. When asked about the episode of exhibiting his genitals, he said he felt guilty about it and considered his hospitalization fair punishment for his sin. In the context of this young man's mode of being-in-the-world, it seemed probable that his genital exhibitionism was another instance of showing what he "had."

From the standpoint of rehabilitation, it was important to understand that this was not a case of sexual perversion, or castration anxiety, or a religious delusion, or rebellion against parental authority, or paranoid schizophrenia. The real issue was inherent in the erroneous overestimation of "having" as constituting *"the way, the truth, and the life"* (Jn. 14:6).

Another case was that of a young woman who sought treatment because a girl friend advised her "to improve her personality." She started out by reserving for herself the right not to speak of certain matters that she considered to be private. After a few sessions it was pointed out to her that even though she was refusing to tell anything specific about herself, the quality of her presence in the therapeutic encounter seemed to indicate a strong concern with being able to hurt people through cunning and connivance.

The patient was noticeably surprised at this, but tried to change the subject. However, gradually she began to reveal a personal history replete with cruelties, deceptions, painful involvements with men and women. Throughout her turbulent, unhappy years until that time, there was noticeable a continuous thread of an overriding conviction that the important thing in life is the mental know-how and capacity "to outsmart and hurt others before they can hurt you." The process of rehabilitating this patient centered around the religious value *"they that take the sword shall perish with the sword"* (Matt. 26:52). Furthermore, she was led to understand the antecedent necessity of "being" before "doing." She was helped to see the meaning and personal relevance of the biblical statement, *"As man thinketh in his heart, so is he"* (Prov. 23:7).

Often the concern with having and doing is combined in the same individual. Such an individual, a middle-aged mother of two children, sought treatment for a variety of psychic and somatic complaints, as well as a particularly difficult marital situation. In the course of treatment, it became evident that she was so imbued with a business outlook on life that she inadvertently endeavored to conduct her marital affairs and motherly duties on the basis of business principles. She was concerned with getting a fair return, profiting, getting quality for her investments. Much of her marital life centered around stormy "balancing of accounts" between herself and her husband.

The rehabilitation process of this patient involved elucidation of the interrelationship between her various difficulties and the misdirected concerns with "having and getting, by being able to

do." The religious values of love, truth, peace, gratitude, participation in existence as a beneficial presence entered very slowly
into her unaccustomed ears and consciousness. At one point,
when confronted with the question of what could free her from
her misdirected concerns, she began by saying, "I guess what
would be important is 'having religion.'" She paused and then
corrected herself, saying, "practicing religion." Eventually, however, she arrived at the conclusion that "being loving" amounts
to "being Godly."

# Transcendence and Healing

Transcendence in its literal meaning signifies stepping over, going beyond, surpassing, being above and beyond. The term *transcendence* is equally a theological as well as a philosophical one. Since existentialism encompasses both theological and philosophical thought, the term *transcendence* has come to play a significant role in existential psychodynamics as a conceptual expression referring to certain distinct epistemological and cognitive phenomena.

The phenomenon of healing is as mysterious and unfathomable in its essence as life itself. Man can destroy life but he cannot make it. He can produce disease but he cannot directly make health. Science can explore the most minute observable details of regenerative processes, but what the essence of healing is eludes the scientific modality of knowledge. Healing, Creativity, Love, Existence are mysteries of Being accessible to human cognition only under special circumstances and conditions. The special circumstances and conditions may reveal themselves in the course of existential psychotherapy as being intrinsically related to those states of consciousness that are here denoted as transcendence.

From a psychotherapeutic standpoint, then, the following definition offers itself: Transcendence is a broadened state of consciousness enabling man to cognize reality in dimensions that are above and beyond dualities and multiplicities.

The following phenomena of transcendence have been found to be significant if healing is to take place in the psychotherapeutic process:

1. transcendence of the subject/object dichotomy between therapist and patient;
2. transcendence of the body/mind dichotomy;

3. transcendence of dualistic thought;
4. transcendence of the ego;
5. transcendence of disease as expression of the pleasure/pain duality;
6. transcendence of causal and teleological thinking;
7. transcendence of the motivational split of means and ends;
8. transcendence of the temporo-spatial coordinates of experience;
9. transcendence of the epistemic barrier between mind and world;
10. transcendence of the duality of being/nonbeing; and
11. transcendence of the separation between man and Ultimate Reality (God).

*No. 1:* In order for the subject/object dichotomy between therapist and patient to be transcended, the therapist must have realized, at least to some appreciable degree, most of the other modalities of transcendence as enumerated above. For only then is he capable of phenomenological perception. Only then is he adequately open and receptive to cognize that which reveals itself. And how does that which reveals itself reveal itself? It reveals itself in the form of happenings. Phenomena are existential events occurring from moment to moment, revealing themselves as shared experiences. Phenomena are continuously affecting all. This is a fact, regardless of whether the participants are aware of the phenomena or not. Phenomena have the quality of transcendence. Heidegger points up the ontological fact that man "is-in-this-world-as-transcendence."[8] In the psychotherapeutic encounter patient and therapist are mutually affecting each other far beyond verbal and sensory stimuli. Under favorable conditions, the healthy phenomena of the therapist prevails over the unhealthy influence of the patient.

However, if the therapist is unaware of the unhealthy phenomena emanating from a patient, he may become sick for the duration of his contact with that patient. This is somewhat reminiscent of what in traditional psychoanalysis is called a transference-countertransference impasse. The problem with that formulation, however, is that it implies a historico-causal-genetic conceptual frame. In the existential psychotherapeutic situation, however, there is a keen awareness of the fact that all conceptual presuppositions (including existentialistic ones) represent obstacles to the realization of the therapeutically essential experience of transcending the subject-object split.

*No. 2:* Transcendence of the body/mind dichotomy leads to an intuitive understanding of "body language." It enables the therapist and the patient to become aware of the subtle messages contained in bodily phenomena as they occur from moment to moment in the course of the psychotherapeutic encounter. The "silent voice" of Existence speaking from the bodies of patient and therapist reveals to them the unity of body and mind. Communication thus becomes truly existential in a hermeneutic[9] sense inasmuch as it consists of authentic elucidation of that which is transpiring from moment to moment.

To illustrate, a psychotherapist became aware of the fact that whenever he was with one of his patients, he had a painful urge to go to the bathroom. Having struggled with himself for a while without being able to understand this phenomenon, he revealed it to his patient and enjoined him to explore the meaning of this experience. Strangely enough, the patient, showing little surprise, remarked that his wife had a similar problem. She habitually wet the bed, especially after arguments, which usually centered around her objections to his rigid self-control and withholding of emotions.

The example illustrates the transcendence of both the subject/object dichotomy and the body/mind dichotomy, since in this particular incident the "silent message" came from the patient's (and his wife's) and the doctor's organisms. Body was revealed as mind, and mind as body. The patient discovered that his body-mind spoke to his wife, and that she responded to him with her body-mind on an organismic level in a rebellious way. The doctor, however, was able to translate the body language into verbal elucidation, and thus the patient's consciousness was broadened in the direction of understanding one aspect of his mode of being-in-the-world.

In another situation a therapist experienced severe pain in his eyes while in the presence of a particular patient. The elucidation of this phenomenon revealed a secret fantasy in the patient, that is, his desires to pluck out the eyes of the doctor, thus appropriating to himself the therapist's supposed capacities "to see into people's minds."

*No. 3:* Dualistic thinking is inherent, on the one hand, in the language, and, on the other, in the misinterpretation of existence in terms of doing and not-doing, having and not-having.

Linguistic logic differentiates four categories of response: yes; no; yes and no; neither yes nor no. Existence, freedom, love, wisdom, understanding, truth, health belong to none of these. To the average person this is unthinkable, since ordinary thinking is silent verbalization. Thought as language cannot go beyond itself. As long as thought is language-bound it must be dualistic. Transcendence of dualistic thinking implies a mode of thinking that is outside, that is, beyond language and symbolic imagery. Such thinking is not an act; it cannot be done or not done. Such thinking happens to man in "choiceless nonevaluative awareness."[10] Heidegger calls it "das Andenkende Denken" in contrast to "das Vorstellende Denken."[11] (The prerequisite for such thinking to come into being is the realization of the limitation of discursive dualistic thought and the condition of *Gelassenheit*, which is best translated "reverent choiceless letting-be of what is, so that it can reveal itself in the essence of its being."[12]) The transcendence of dualistic thinking is then a state of consciousness characterized by an openness and receptivity to that mysterious flash of light which constitutes understanding. Understanding is seeing what really is. It is the revelation of truth from moment to moment. Truth liberates. Healing requires the tranquillity of the free mind.

*No. 4:* This brings us to the fourth point, namely, the transcendence of the ego. It is an eminently significant phenomenon that in moments of understanding, there is no understander. In moments of true experiencing, there is no experiencer. The understander or experiencer emerges immediately after the event and promptly proceeds to evaluate, categorize, and use that which has been understood, experienced, revealed. The ego, then, as we speak about it here, is a certain mental activity, in the sense of doing or not-doing and having or not-having. As long as this mental activity is in the foreground of estimation, it interferes with that openness and receptivity which are prerequisite for understanding to happen. In other words, clinging to concepts and symbols of oneself in terms of a functional capacity or possession of any sort (for example, material, ideological, spiritual, educational) is a form of mental bondage and "idolatry" that hampers the capacity to see what is. Ignorance is that mental activity which ignores what really is. Seeing the ego as an obstacle to seeing leads to its transcendence. In order to see what is, the mind must transcend its preoccupation with what should be. Karen Horney's concept of the ego-ideal[13] expresses such mental attachment to certain symbols of what should be, which then dislocates the patient's consciousness from its actual existential ground, thus leading to alienation. Carl Jung is quoted as having said that modern man is like someone who lives on the twentieth floor of a house that begins at the tenth floor; below, there is nothing.

No. 5: Disease entails suffering. Pain becomes identified with disease. The dualistically thinking mind is inclined to conclude that the alternative to pain is pleasure. Pleasure, therefore, tends to be considered the expression of health. This leads to the hedonistic misinterpretation of health, with its concomitant quest for pleasure as a means to an end. We are reminded of some "scientific" theories postulating that anhedonia (pleasure deficiency) is etiologically significant in schizophrenic disorders. Suffering man tends to become involved in the dualistic preoccupation with pain and pleasure. The dualism of pain and pleasure tends to become the central issue in a patient's thinking. Such mental entanglement leads to a vicious cycle and to aggravation of suffering. Disease cannot be resolved from this standpoint because pleasure is intrinsically connected with pain, and vice versa, somewhat like two sides of the same coin. Transcendence of the pleasure/pain duality leads to a state of consciousness that is receptive to the truth about the personal meaning of disease rather than being caught up in the agitated search for the avoidance of pain and the quest for health through pleasure. It is truth that heals, not the escape from suffering. Understanding of disease leads to health, not the pursuit of pleasure. Health is neither gratification nor frustration; it is Ontic Integration,[14] resulting from reverent mindfulness and responsiveness to Existence as the ontological Ground. In other words, health is not a matter of feeling good or feeling bad; it is not a matter of feelings. Health is "at-one-ment" with what really is. The following example illustrates the dilemma of pleasure-pain involvement, or the preoccupation with feeling good or feeling bad.

A patient was in the habit of touching his nose occasionally during his sessions. When this was brought to his attention, he said, "Why shouldn't I relieve myself if my nose is itching?" The therapist answered, "If you were not in such a hurry to find relief, maybe the meaning of your nose-itching could reveal itself." The patient then began to restrain himself from scratching his nose. As he did so, the itch became worse, almost intolerable. The patient was in conflict and felt frustrated. At this point, it was

brought to his attention that if he is scratching he cannot understand the meaning of the itch, because by scratching he combats
it, that is, he is in conflict with it. However, by not scratching he
is also in conflict with it, because he is restraining himself. As long
as he is in conflict with the itching of his nose, he cannot understand it. The truth can only reveal itself to him if he is neither
scratching nor not-scratching, that is, if he allows the itch to take
place without being for or against it. When the patient thus
reached a reverent letting-be attitude toward the itching of his
nose, he suddenly observed that a thought passed through his
mind: "I wish I could deceive him." At this moment he blushed,
but the itching ceased. Thus, the patient's mind became aware of
itself. Knowledge of truth freed him from the vicious cycle of pleasure and pain, or gratification and frustration.

*No. 6:* Causal and teleological thinking is calculative-discursive
activity of the mind that, while it may produce impressive theories and formulations, nevertheless cannot lead to healing. Knowing about oneself is not the same as knowing oneself. Knowing
oneself in the past or in the future is conceptual and theoretical.
Since human existence is a process, man cannot know himself
once and for all. Knowing oneself denotes a state of cognitive
integration based on enteroceptive, kinesthetic, exteroceptive, and
cognitive awareness. This means that in order to know himself,
man must transcend his causal and teleological modes of thinking and become capable of such awareness as would enable him
to be in harmony with that existential process that he is. Knowing oneself is then a paradox; it is not really possible in a direct
way. Knowing oneself is knowing the unreality of the self. Vision
becomes aware of itself by seeing. Man knows himself by understanding what is. When consciousness is capable of seeing what
is, man becomes what he really is.

*No. 7:* Transcendence of the motivational split means the following: Under ordinary conditions man tends to think in terms of
gratifying his desires. In general, he is mostly concerned with
achieving certain ends or results that would profit him. He thus
becomes divided between what is and what should be. That which
is becomes for him a means toward what should be. The moment
this motivational dichotomy enters into his interhuman existential sphere, he becomes a victim of his own tendencies to victim-
ize people by using them as means to an end. The person whose
thinking is entangled in this dualistic split of means and ends is

unable to understand his fellow man. His life becomes a series of misunderstandings and conflicts. In this "ways and means" mode of existence there is a source of interhuman friction leading to severe disturbances and much suffering. Transcendence of the motivational split of means and ends leads to a realization that human understanding, harmony, love, and contentment are only possible when there is reverence for the human being as existent, which can be neither a means nor an end with impunity. Erich Fromm has dealt with this problem extensively in a chapter on "the marketing orientation."[15]

*No. 8:* Ordinarily, thinking is time bound. Thinking usually proceeds in terms of the past, moving through the present, toward the future. Thinking consists of juggling past experiences and information, which constitute memories, and projecting them into the future in anticipation of what is to come. Or, the present is evaluated in the light of past experiences and future anticipations. What, in traditional psychoanalytic therapy, is called insight is really nothing else than hindsight. Hindsight is knowledge about "what was" in order to change "what shall be" in accordance with "what should be." Hindsight is a means to an end. It is based on the illusion that man can change himself by willing it. However, man cannot really change himself. Change happens to man in the open receptiveness to what is. The moment-to-moment realization of "what is" transforms man. True insight, then, is continuous awareness of Existence as an infinite stream of events. For, as long as the mind is time bound, it is closed to the unexpected, the new, the creative discovery, and the creative response. In order for healing to occur, there must be openness and receptivity for the unknown to reveal itself as understanding. This requires the transcendence of the temporo-spatial coordinates of experience, which reveals the timeless now. Understanding is a nontemporal "flash of light."

*No. 9:* The epistemic barrier[16] connotes a certain obstacle to direct cognition that is universally present in man to various degrees, depending upon the intensity with which he clings to concepts and symbols in his mind. A rose is a rose is a rose. No matter how many times we say it, the fact is that we do not see the rose because the concept "rose" is in the way. Conceptual and symbolic frames of reference are those walls that isolate Freudian psychoanalysts from Adlerians, Adlerians from Jungians, and pseudoexistentialists from other pseudoexistentialists. Perhaps the most important and most difficult postulate of existentialism is the transcendence of the epistemic barrier. Such transcendence is attained through genuine existential, that is, experiential realization of the painfulness of being a prisoner in one's own mental isolation cell. The mind that transcends its own epistemic barrier becomes capable of true communion with what really is. The universal human inclination to get stuck or become attached to symbols is the basis for man's inherently idolatrous nature with its tragic consequences that have been known since biblical times. To transcend the epistemic barrier means to see beyond the symbol. It entails the realization that symbols are but road signs pointing the way beyond themselves. The idolatrous man is like a traveler who, on his way to New York, settles down in the first motel named New York, and believes that he has arrived. Symbols are products of man's desire to give form to that which forever must remain formless. *"I AM THAT I AM,"* said God to Moses (Ex. 3:14). We understand this to mean "I am that which forever Is" or "I am that which really Is."

The epistemic barrier is easily discernible in the eyes of some patients; they look "deaf." "Deaf eyes" communicate an unwillingness to hear. With the aid of the therapist, it is possible for a patient to "learn to see his own eyes without looking into the mirror." He can also develop the capacity to be aware of having "blind ears." "Blind ears" communicate a refusal to "see the point" that someone is making. The epistemic barrier reveals itself as the phenomena of "deaf eyes" and "blind ears." When this awareness happens, transcendence of the epistemic barrier has occurred. The open mind is attained through genuine experiential realization of the closed mind. Socrates' wisdom came from knowing his own not-knowing. There is a famous Zen story about a certain person who, in the moment of enlightenment, exclaimed, "The bottom of the pail has broken through!" This was to express the sudden opening of the mind that hitherto was closed by clinging to its contents.

*No. 10:* On the level of ego-consciousness, man is forever seeking the confirmation of his existence. He strives to "constitute himself," as one patient put it, by "being" good or by "being" bad; by "being" important or by "being" needed. However, since the need to confirm one's being is in itself evidence of doubts concerning its reality, man is caught up in a situation in which not only does he have a need to seek confirmation of his own being, but he also has a need to deny this need. The above-mentioned patient—whose striving for "self-constitution" took the form of "being" in a continuous state of marital discord with his wife—once exclaimed, "But by the very fact of seeking to constitute myself, I negate myself!" At this moment, he realized that his dread of nonbeing drove him to crave being.[17] The fear of facing one's own dread of nonbeing is expressed as dread of dread. As long as human consciousness is preoccupied with being and nonbeing, conflicts are of central importance. For in conflicts sensations are generated, through which the notion of being gains sensory confirmation. When there is neither the pleasure nor the pain of conflict, being seeks to confirm itself by thinking, which also can be sensed. "Cogito, ergo sum." When there is neither sensory stimulation nor thinking, there is a void that conjures up the dread of nonbeing. The dualistic entanglements in the problem of being and nonbeing is that state of ignorance which is the perennial source of suffering. From this perspective, disease and suffering are revealed as the unceasing desire to confirm being and negate nonbeing. The tragic element of the human condition is rooted in that cognitive deficiency which underlies the desire of man to confirm himself as primary reality. The dilemma of the being/nonbeing duality and the endless vicissitudes connected with escaping the awareness of it, can only be resolved through the transcendence of being and nonbeing. This implies a cognitive realization of Existence as a reality that is neither being nor nonbeing. It is therefore a Transcendental Reality manifesting itself in the universe and in human experience as Love-Intelligence.

How does such cognitive realization of Existence as a Transcendental Reality come about? The desire for self-confirmation arises when man feels ignored or inconsequential in this world. This generates existential anxiety, which, in turn, seeks comfort in self-confirmatory action. However, every confirmation of being is simultaneously its negation. Consequently, this is a futile and painfully self-defeating endeavor. Self-confirmation is always self-destruction, and vice versa. Viewed in this light, even suicide appears to be a desperate act of ultimate self-confirmation. As long as there is a need to confirm one's being, there are psychopathology and somatic concomitants. Conversely, as long as there is psychopathology and suffering, there is ignorance concerning being and nonbeing. Seeing ignorance as ignorance is enlightening. Transcendence is enlightened consciousness.

*No. 11:* When all previously described modes of transcendence are existentially realized, man becomes capable of cognizing Ultimate Reality. It is revealed to him in personal experience as the nondual realm of Love-Intelligence. Transcendent consciousness is conscious of Love as that Intelligence which forever reveals itself as Understanding. Love is here revealed as a mode of cognition, and man as an instrument, a medium, an image, a likeness or reflection of it. This no doubt corresponds to what theologians call the moment when God becomes real to man. This is what Job must have meant when he said, *"I have heard of thee by the hearing of the ear; but now mine eye seeth Thee"* (Job 42:5). And Job was healed.

# Existential Psychotherapy:
# Basic Principles

In his 1961 address to the plenary session of the Third World Congress of Psychiatry, Jules Masserman pointed out that anxiety in man is centered around three major concerns: first, his physical integrity; second, his social integration; and third, whether he may be nothing more than a "cosmic triviality."

Existentialism emphasizes the importance of this third concern and points to the fact that it is exactly the capacity for such concern which particularly distinguishes man from all other living creatures. Therefore, any attempt at understanding man must of necessity take this special "gift" of human consciousness into consideration.

Existential psychotherapy, therefore, views man primarily from an ontic perspective.[18] It considers man's harmony or disharmony with existence to be of primary significance and views pathology as both manifestation and consequence of man's failure to be that which he truly is.

Since the objective of existential psychotherapy is the "discovery" of the authentic individual,[19] it follows quite understandably that the primary qualification of the psychotherapist must be his own freedom from artificiality, technicity, and preconceived theoretic dogmatisms (including existentialism as mere philosophy). This does not mean that he must be uninformed and untrained. On the contrary, he must be so familiar with most schools of thought as to remain unhampered by a tendency to cling to any particular frame of reference for a subjective sense of comfort, security and guidance. It can be said, therefore, that an existential psychotherapist must be free from technical concerns (somewhat as a good musician might be while playing, say, Bach). Transcendence

123

of the need for technique makes it possible for a genuine encounter to occur between doctor and patient.

Encounter is a special feature of the therapist-patient relationship in existential psychotherapy. Its essential spontaneity and lack of structure makes it possible for the patient to reveal his mode of being-in-the-world without premeditation or interference by the therapist. The therapist, in turn, being free of the encumbrances that theoretical and technologic considerations tend to pose, is enabled to perceive "what really is" phenomenologically. Having thus perceived that which reveals itself, he is able to "shed light" on it. This activity is not so much interpretative as phenomenologically elucidating (*phaos* = light, *apophansis* = statement, language).

The perspective of the existential psychotherapist is neither objective nor subjective, neither personal nor interpersonal. It is, rather, transpersonal, a perspective that requires a capacity for cognitive transcendence to be realized by both the therapist and the patient. Cognitive transcendence means that the therapist's and the patient's concern is with the truth as it reveals itself through man. For man does not produce truth; he manifests it and is defined by it. The capacity for cognitive transcendence is realized through a process of freeing the mind of its epistemic prison. Thus, the liberation of consciousness from ingrained categories of thought is an important aspect of the existential therapeutic process.

In the course of existential psychotherapy, patient and therapist partake, again and again, of the experiential realization that truth liberates, understanding (that is, seeing) transforms, and love heals. Consequently, the essential concern of the therapist and the patient is to understand (that is, see) truth as it emerges within a climate of love.

Significantly, patients initially find it most difficult to be truly concerned with truth, understanding, and love, even though they quite readily pay lip service to them. Tacitly, however, they tend to consider these issues idealistic and somewhat irrelevant to practical existence, well-being, and mental health.

However, in the course of the therapeutic process it becomes quite evident that love, understanding and truth are fundamental, essential issues of existence because the unfolding and realization of human potentialities hinges upon them. The loving state of consciousness enables the mind to realize its optimum cognitive potentialities. Understanding makes it possible for man to commune meaningfully with his fellow man. Truth, in turn, liberates man from his past and makes him fully available for the present.

It follows that existential psychotherapy is neither causalistic, historical, genetic, etiologic nor teleological. It is mainly epistemological in its focus, which means that it seeks to benefit man through the optimal unfoldment of his cognitive capacities.

In the course of the existential therapeutic process the historical, causal, genetic, and teleological aspects of individual human existences tend to emerge into consciousness spontaneously and be cognized implicitly rather than explicitly. *On ne guerit pas en se souvenant mais on se souvient en guerissant* (One does not heal by remembering but one remembers as a result of healing).

As mentioned above, existential psychotherapy is viewed as a process of cognitive unfoldment. Aspects of the patient's authentic individuality that have been hidden, covered up, obstructed, undeveloped become gradually unveiled, liberated from the fog of pretensions. For, everyday life proceeds largely in the realm of inventions; that is, everyday life is not really lived but "conducted" along routine, preconceived lines and assumptions of what "should be" and what "should not be." Mental assumptions tend to become more important than reality and to hamper human consciousness in its cognitive function. The process of discovering the authentic being consists of uncovering, dispelling the "inventions" that mask and cover the truth of what really is.

The existential therapist's characteristic attitude expresses the principle of "letting be" (not to be confused with leaving alone). Letting-be[20] is open-minded, wakeful receptivity to that which reveals itself without interference. It is the manifestation of reverence and love in the process of paying attention to understand the truth of what really is from moment to moment. Letting-be may seem trivial, yet it is actually the most difficult aspect of existential psychotherapy, as most trainees will readily admit. While leaving alone is an interpersonal act, letting-be is neither an act nor interpersonal; it is a state of consciousness.

Wakeful receptivity is a mode of human functioning that eludes both the categories of activity and passivity. It is neither active nor passive. Wakeful receptivity is the precondition for understanding to happen. For understanding cannot be produced.

Understanding is a cognitive event. That which is understood needs no interpretation. It speaks for itself. Human suffering and despair are mostly conditioned by deficiencies in man's capacity to understand. The discovery of the true nature of understanding often relieves man of his tragic inclination to pride himself arrogantly on discursive knowledge, and to confuse explanations or interpretations with true understanding. The very understanding of the nature of understanding tends to transform man and make him more humble. The open mind is attained through experiencing of the closed mind. Open-minded, wakeful receptivity to the truth as it reveals itself in the encounter between therapist and patient proceeds in the here and now of the absolute present.

Since most patients tend to be time-bound, however, the present is to a great extent but a reverberation of the past. To be the "captive of time," that is, to have a problem of temporality, means to be hampered in one's freedom to respond to what truly is because of the habit of evaluating the present in the light of the past and the conjectured future. For most patients the words of Ecclesiastes (3:15) have much validity: *"That which hath been is now, and that which is to be hath already been."* For the therapist in turn, the final sentence of the same quotation carries the therapeutic message: *"And God requireth that which is past."* To be free and in harmony with the flux of life, man must cease clutching at the past. He must become open, receptive, and fully responsive (responsible) to the present.

Since man, from an ontological viewpoint, is seen as a "translucent medium of Existence,"[21] it follows that the definition of the *summum bonum,* the optimal good, differs from the prevailing concern. In our culture, that concern is successful "functioning" in order to master the world (through conquest). The existential view is that man can become complete (whole, holy, healed) only by finding a way to live in reverent, loving harmony, that is, at-one-ment with the world of which he is inescapably a part.

Consequently, the prevailing concern of existentialism is the realization of the loving mode of being-in-the-world. The realization of at-one-ment and love as a mode of being-in-the-world tends to relieve man from problems of spatiality. The term *spatiality* is related to the fact that the subject/object dichotomy requires human consciousness to take into account space as an existential coordinate. Consequently, spatial aspects of life situations may at times assume problematic character, as in agoraphobia, in some compulsive neuroses, or psychotic distortions of body image and space perception.

The reader may at this point ask: And what about transference, countertransference, resistance, dream interpretation, libido, psychosexual development, unconscious conflict? What about nosology and differential diagnosis, psychodynamics, symbolism, genital primacy? What about psychic mechanisms, infantile amnesia, ego psychology, archetypes, conditional reflexes? What about neurophysiology and psycho-pharmacology?

The answer to these questions is that while the sum total of partial phenomena never adds up to a whole, and while the whole of man can never be understood in parts, nevertheless the thorough study of the partial aspects of man seems warranted and necessary. Existential psychotherapy does not reject the partial phenomena. Interestingly enough, when viewed in the broader context of existence, these phenomena tend to assume new and somewhat different meanings. In actual therapeutic practice, however, they seldom require explicit utilization. As far as the patient is concerned, the therapeutic process is a holistic and primarily epistemological-existential experience.

The realization of harmony with existence, that is, ontic integration, does not fail to be reflected in favorable social adaptability as well as in improved organismic-biological functioning. Healing is a manifestation of existence. *Medicus curat, natura sanat* (The physician treats, but nature heals).

## THE THERAPEUTIC PROCESS

The psychotherapeutic session is a segment of life. Life is an event in time. Existence is manifested through man somewhat as light becomes visible while passing through a translucent medium. Man partakes in existence; he does not cause it to be. If he, however, comes to fancy himself as the "maker" or "master" of existence, he invariably runs into conflict with the fundamental order of things. He finds himself in disharmony with the ontological conditions of existence.

Thinking in terms of *techniques* of psychotherapy—or of "doing" psychotherapy—poses a similar problem, for it, too, fails to consider the fact that existence is an event. The idea of "managing" or "handling" cases in psychotherapy represents an objectification that violates the essence of man as an existential phenomenon.

Since man is never just a "case," psychotherapy—strictly speaking—cannot be "done."

Psychotherapy, as life itself, is an event in time. It is a process. Patients appear in the psychotherapeutic situation, as in all human encounters, not only as samples of various psychic mechanisms or disease entities, but, above and beyond that, as people with specific ways of experiencing and cognizing life, specific ways of responding to stimuli, and specific ways of responding to deep stirrings of inner potentialities that demand realization within a limited but unknown time span.[22]

The event of the existential encounter, however, as mentioned above, is phenomenologically characterized by a transcendence of the temporo-spatial coordinates of existence;[23] this means that in the existential encounter itself, the experience of the passage of time and the awareness of separation between subject and object are absent.

Phenomena are manifestations of existence. Man's awareness of the phenomena is obscured and limited by his strivings to impose his will upon what is. His pursuit of what "should be" tends to make him unaware of the phenomena as they occur. Therefore, a therapeutic process cannot be conducted, intended, managed; it must be allowed to occur.

The essence of existential communication[24] lies in its nonteleological character. In the light of this, the concept "free association" is revealed as a misnomer containing a double contradiction: first, it is not free because it is intended to be free; second, it is not free because it serves a purpose.

To understand himself man needs to be understood. By being understood he learns to understand. When two people share in understanding, they experience communion. Communion is that union which makes differentiation possible. Man becomes an individual through participation. By losing himself in participation, he finds himself as a "presence"; individuals are wholly similar and wholly different at the same time, just as mosaic pictures may contain similar stone fragments but be entirely different in their overall design.

In the moment of being understood, patients experience communion, that is, they experience a release from epistemic isolation. The subject/object dichotomy between patient and therapist melts away. This is in marked contradistinction to being given an interpretation, which is often experienced as an accusation, an attack, or even condemnation.

When striving and intending are recognized as self-defeating therapeutic attitudes, there is a tendency to conclude that passivity might be a desirable one. This, however, is a mistake, since striving to be active and striving to be passive are the same. This points up the futility of the perennial disputes between the so-called active therapists and the adherents to the traditionally passive approaches. The issue is neither activity nor passivity, neither directiveness nor nondirectiveness, but awareness, that is, being in a condition of wakeful receptivity and responsiveness to the phenomena. This condition of being is vitiated by striving and intending, evaluating, judging, categorizing, and pigeonholing into conceptual schemes and psychodynamic patterns. Freud, interestingly enough, wrote about this problem quite clearly:

> For as soon as attention is deliberately concentrated in a certain degree, one begins to select from the material before one; one point will be fixed in mind with particular clearness and some other consequently disregarded, and in this selection one's expectations or inclinations will be followed. This is just what must not be done, however; if one's expectations are followed in this selection there is a danger of never finding anything but what is already known, and if one follows one's inclinations anything which is to be perceived will most certainly be falsified.[25]

Freud recommended the attitude of "free floating attention." It is of great significance that his recommendation was interpreted as passivity. This is easily understood, however, if we consider our propensity to dualistic thinking.

Heidegger spoke of "letting be," which he described as a relationship in which all that is can reveal itself in the essence of its being. Essence is the inner potentiality of something existing. Truth can only reveal itself under conditions of freedom. Freedom is letting-be; therefore, the essence of truth is freedom.[26]

Letting-be must not be mistaken for quietism, passivity, nondirectiveness, or leaving alone. The concept of letting-be means affirmation of the existence of another person. It connotes an attitude that favors the free emergence of the inherent creative potentialities of all. Letting-be expresses a therapeutic attitude of the highest ethical order inasmuch as it refrains from treating the patient as an object of exploration and manipulation, but relates itself to the patient as an existent in an affirmative and perceptive way. Affirmation of a person's freedom to be what he is, is an act of love. Love is reverence. Being with a person in the spirit of letting-be makes it possible to comprehend this person in a transjective, that is, experiential way. The experience of being thus understood is therapeutically beneficial in itself.

The existential psychotherapist does not try to "do" psychotherapy; he lives it. He meets his patient in the openness of an interhuman existential encounter. He does not seek to make interpretations; he does not evaluate and judge. He allows what is to be, so that it can reveal itself in the essence of its being, and proceeds to elucidate what he has understood. In contrast to the interpretative approach, this is a "hermeneutic," that is, clarifying, mode of being with a patient.[27]

Nonevaluative awareness of what is leads to an understanding of the patient's mode of being-in-the-world with an elucidation of the implications for his existence. Complete understanding of one's mode of being tends to bring about a shift in world view, that is, a changed attitude toward life. Change occurs the moment man can see the totality of his situation. Change is the result of expanding consciousness. It is to be emphasized that, contrary to general belief, man cannot change himself; change happens to man. Darkness cannot be removed from a room; it vanishes when light enters.

It seems, therefore, useless to claim or to aspire to cure patients. Healing occurs through a meaningful shift in the world view of an individual, brought about through genuine understanding of the structure of his existence. As already mentioned, understanding is an event that happens in the openness of the existential encounter. Understanding is a modality of cognition that constitutes the essence of love. This love is a condition of being, in the presence of which constructive events have the freedom to occur.[28]

Thus, the existential psychotherapeutic process can be described as a meeting of two or more beings in openness and wakeful receptivity to what is, leading to a broadening of consciousness through revelation of that which hitherto has been obscured. The broadening of consciousness and the capacity to see what is, bring man into harmony with life. Personality integration becomes an expression of ontic integration.[29]

The existential therapeutic action is neither operational nor explorative, nor reconstructive, nor interpretative, nor directive, nor nondirective; it is experiential and hermeneutic, that is, clarifying. Since it is phenomenological and transcendental, that is, since the mode of cognition is such that the subject/object dichotomy is transcended, the so-called psychic mechanisms of transference, countertransference, projection, introjection, identification, resistance, empathy, etc., lose much of their significance. The patient participates as a total human being, not as ego, id, and superego. He is an existent in encounter with another. His relationship with the therapist is expressed by Buber[30] as "mutual spiritual inclusion," by Marcel[31] as "intersubjectivity," by Heidegger[32] as "being-in-the-world-as-transcendence" and by Rogers[33] as "total presence" (which he describes as total organismic sensitivity to the other person). From our standpoint, however, as mentioned above, the nature of the therapeutic relationship could best be characterized as transpersonal.

The therapeutic process moves in the temporality which is absolutely real, and that is the eternal present. The present contains the past. The proper elucidation of the present reveals the past. This, however, is only a by-product and is of secondary significance.

The capacity to be aware of the experiential impact of the environment upon one, and vice versa, tends to open up a dimension of consciousness that leads to a growing understanding of one's own structure of being-in-this-world or failing to-be-in-this-world because of various defensive attitudes and strivings. As one patient put it: "I can feel myself standing in my own way. I understand how isolated and lonely I am."

The experiential awareness of one's own defensiveness converts the meaning of the defenses from comfort to obstacle and impediment. The moment one experiences one's strivings and avidity as sources of stress, anxiety, and conflict, one becomes aware of their self-defeating nature.

The ontological essence and existential meaning of a communication or dream are to be found primarily in the experiencing of its basic existential context and only secondarily in its symbolic content. A young man reported the following dream:

I was surrounded by wasps. I tried not to bother them in the hope that they might not bother me. I tried to remain as immobile as possible. When one wasp settled on my eyelid, I was seized with panic and didn't dare to move lest it would sting me through the lid and reach my eye—that is, "I"—I felt in a real jam. Had I moved, I would have gotten stung. Had I not moved, I would have gotten stung anyway. The anxiety was unbearable. Just at that point where I couldn't stand it any longer, I woke up.

The elucidation of the meaning of this dream led this patient to realize that defensiveness is seldom warranted, whether it is active or passive. He concluded that the best solution is to wake up and understand that what we are mostly defending are our preconceptions, that is, dreams about ourselves. Defending one's dream is just more dreaming.

One patient was so sensitive to coercive and demanding people that she habitually reacted to them with breathing difficulties, depression, and states of depersonalization. Having understood her reactions to be of defensive character, she made a surprising remark: "I wish I were a glass window pane!" At first it was not clear what she meant. But from that day on she began to let go of her defensiveness and began to allow coercive stimuli to pass through herself somewhat as light passes through a window pane. She remained perceptive of the nature of the stimuli, but having ceased to defend herself against them, became immune to them. Interestingly enough, some time later, when reminded of her strange remark, she said: "A window pane is really a good symbol for a human being. It is brittle, easily destroyed, yet enduring. Its function is to be translucent, to shed light. The cleaner it is, the more invisible it is, and yet the more light it sheds. The dirtier it gets, the more ego it acquires; the more visible it becomes itself, the less light it sheds."

Cognition and consciousness are fundamental criteria of mental health, and along with authenticity of being, they constitute the central issues in existential psychotherapy. Another patient's prevailing attitude toward the therapist was provocatively hostile. After a while he realized the futility of his strivings and changed his attitude to a friendly, ingratiatingly cooperative one, only to discover to his surprise that it made no difference in what manner he strived to "get at" his therapist. For as long as he was striving to be good or bad, to agree or disagree, to oppose or cooperate, he

EXISTENTIAL PSYCHOTHERAPY        133

had a closed mind. His state of consciousness was such that his cognitive faculties were impaired.

In contradistinction to the traditional psychoanalytic interest in the content of unconscious motivation and its historical context, existential psychoanalysis points to the epistemological problem which arises as a result of the mind's tendency to attach itself to mental images and motivations in general. In existential psychotherapy the content of the mental preoccupation, or attachment, or striving is secondary. The primary issue is the disturbance of consciousness that results from it.

> For as man is, so is his cognition;
> and as man's cognition is, so is he.[34]

# Notes

1. Pierre Teilhard de Chardin, *The Human Phenomenon* (New York: Harper Torchbook, 1961).

2. Martin Heidegger, *Sein und zeit* (Tübingen: Max Neimeyer Verlag, 1953).

3. James Legge, *The Texts of Taoism* (New York: Julian Press, 1959).

4. R. M. Osborn, "The Inward Light," *The Friend* 26, no. 64 (Winter-Spring 1963).

5. Thomas Hora, "Beyond Self," paper delivered at the annual conference on existential psychiatry of the American Ontoanalytical Association, New York, December 1960.

6. D. T. Suzuki, *The Doctrine of No-mind* (London: Rider, 1949).

7. D. T. Suzuki, "The Mirage of Pathology," paper delivered at the International Congress of Psychiatry, Montreal, June 1961.

8. Heidegger, *Sein und zeit.*

9. Ludwig Biswanger, *Grundformen und erkentniss menschlichen daseins* (Zurich: Max Neihans Verlag, 1942).

10. Jiddu Krishnamurti, *Commentaries on Living* (New York: Harper, 1956).

11. Martin Heidegger, *Unterwegs zur sprache* (Pfuellingen: Guenther Neske, 1959).

12. Martin Heidegger, *Gelassenheit* (Pfuellingen: Guenther Neske, 1959).

13. Karen Horney, *Neurosis and Human Growth* (New York: W. W. Norton, 1950).

14. Thomas Hora, "Ontic Integration," paper delivered at the International Congress of Psychotherapy, Barcelona, September 1958.

15. Erich Fromm, *Man for Himself: An Inquiry into the Psychology of Ethics* (New York: Rinehart & Co., 1947).

16. Thomas Hora, "Epistemological Aspects of Existence and Psychotherapy," *Journal of Individual Psychology* 15 (November 1959), 166-73.

17. Paul Tillich, *The Courage to Be* (New Haven, Conn.: Yale University Press, 1956).

18. Thomas Hora, "Ontic Perspectives in Psychoanalysis," *American Journal of Psychoanalysis* 19, no. 2 (1959), 134-42.

19. Ludwig Biswanger, *Der mensch in der psychiatrie* (Pfuelligen: Guenther Neske, 1957).

20. Heidegger, *Gelassenheit.*

21. Heidegger, *Sein und zeit.*

22. Eugène Minkowski, *Le temps vecu* (Paris: J. L. L. d'Artrey, 1953).

23. Eugène Minkowski, "Encounter and Dialogue," paper delivered at the International Congress of Psychotherapy, Barcelona, September 1958.

24. Thomas Hora, "Existential Communication and Psychotherapy," *Psychoanalysis* 5 (1957).

25. Sigmund Freud, *Collected Papers,* vol. 2 (London: Hogarth Press, 1924).

26. Martin Heidegger, *Existence and Being* (Chicago: Regnery, 1949).

27. Biswanger, *Grundformen und erkentniss menschlichen daseins.*

28. Thomas Hora, "Spiritual Love and Mental Health," paper delivered at the World Congress of Mental Health, Paris, 1961.

29. Hora, "Ontic Integration."

30. Martin Buber, *Between Man and Man* (Boston: Beacon Press, 1955).

31. Gabriel Marcel, *The Philosophy of Existence* (London: Harvill, 1948).

32. Heidegger, *Sein und zeit.*

33. Carl Rodgers, "Persons or Science? A Philosophical Question," *American Journal of Psychology* (1955).

34. W. S. Haas, *The Destiny of the Mind* (New York: Macmillan, 1956).

# Subject Index

# Scripture Index

# Publications by Thomas Hora
## Relating to the Psychiatric Implications of Existentialism

"Beyond Countertransference." *American Journal of Psychotherapy* 10, no. 1 (January 1956).

"Contribution to the Phenomenology of the Supervisory Process." *American Journal of Psychotherapy* 10, no. 4 (October 1957).

"The Role of Group Psychotherapy in the Rehabilitation Process of the Borderline Schizophrenic Patient." *International Journal of Group Psychotherapy* (October 1957).

"Group Psychotherapy, Human Values, and Mental Health. *International Journal of Group Psychotherapy* (April 1958).

"Existential Communication and Psychotherapy." *Psychoanalysis* 5, no. 4 (December 1957).

"The Schizophrenic Patient in the Therapy Group." *Journal of the Hillside Hospital* 8, no. 2 (April 1958).

"Existential Group Psychotherapy." *American Journal of Psychotherapy* 13, no. 1 (January 1959).

"Psychotherapy, Existence, and Religion." *Psychoanalysis and Psychoanalytic Review* 46, no. 2 (Summer 1959).

"Epistemological Aspects of Existence and Psychotherapy." *Journal of Individual Psychology* 1, no. 15 (November 1959).

"Ontic Perspectives in Psychoanalysis." *American Journal of Psychoanalysis* 19, no. 2 (1959).

"The Process of Existential Psychotherapy." Abstract from *Existential Inquiries* 1, no. 1 (1959).

"Tao, Zen, and Existential Psychotherapy." *Psychologia* 2. Kyoto (1959).

"Group Psychotherapy and the Human Condition." *Acta Psychotherapeutica Zurich* 7 (1959).

"Transcendence and Healing." *Journal of Existential Psychiatry* 1, no. 9 (1961).

"The Process of Existential Psychotherapy." *Psychiatric Quarterly* 34 (July 1960).

"Existential Psychiatry and Group Psychotherapy." *American Journal of Psychoanalysis* 21, no. 1 (1961).

"On Meeting a Zen Master Socially." *Psychologia* 4, no. 2 (June 1961), 73-75.

"The Epistemology of Love." *Journal of Existential Psychiatry* 2, no. 7 (Winter 1962).

"Cognition and Health." *Journal of Religion and Health* (April 1962).

"No. 8" and "No. 16." In *Psychoanalysis and Existential Philosophy*, ed. Hendrik M. Ruitenbeek (1962).

"Elements of Ontoanalysis." *Newsletter of Western Society for Existential Psychology and Psychiatry* 1, no. 1 (1962).

"Existential Psychotherapy." In *Current Therapies,* vol. 2, ed. Jules Masserman. New York: Grune & Stratton, 1962.

"Beyond Self." *Psychologia 5*, no. 2 (June 1962).

"The Dynamism of Assumptions." *Problems in Psychotherapy*, vol. 4, 32-36. New York: Karger, Basel, 1963.

"Responsibility." *Review of Existential Psychology and Psychiatry* 2, no. 3 (Fall 1962).

"The Transpersonal Perspective." *American Journal of Psychoanalysis* 23, no. 1 (May 1963).

"Discussion of Dr. Hulbeck's Paper, Three Creative Phases in Psychoanalysis." *American Journal of Psychoanalysis* 23, no. 2 (November 1963).

"Religious Values in Illness and Health." *Journal of Religion and Health* 2, no. 3 (April 1963).

If you would like to obtain other books and tapes
of Thomas Hora's or information about related
publications, please contact us at:

**The PAGL Bookstore**
P.O. Box 4001
Old Lyme, CT 06371
Tel: (860) 434–2999
Fax: (860) 434–1512
PAGLBooks@aol.com
www.pagl.org